T0161157

MY

GIFT

MY
GIFT

*17 Powerful Insights to
Becoming the Best You*

Mark P. Mitchell

Clovercroft/Publishing

My Gift

Published by Clovercroft Publishing, Franklin, Tennessee

All Scripture quotations are taken from the Holy Bible, New International Version®, NIV® Copyright ©1973, 1978, 1984, 2011 by Biblica, Inc.® Used by permission. All rights reserved worldwide.

Edited by OnFire Books

Copy Edit by Christy Callahan

Cover Design by Nelly Sanchez

Interior Design by Suzanne Lawing

Printed in the United States of America

978-1-949572-87-2

To my girls, Makayla and Mallory.
All my love to you both on life's journey.
Dad

*The key to immortality is first living
a life worth remembering.*
—Bruce Lee

Contents

Life Balance, Inspiration, and Health

Acknowledgments

So many people helped to make this book possible!

The book you are about to read could not have come to life without the input, influence, coordination, and participation in my life experiences of so many people. The final inspiration to get going came from a conversation with my amazing wife, Gina.

For sure, I couldn't have pulled it together without the support and partnership of the OnFire Books team, led by my friend Tammy Kling and her awesome team, including Tiarra Tompkins, Mark Nolan, and for sure others behind the scene.

Without a doubt, my parents, Phil and Nancy Mitchell, have been the greatest influence in my life from the moment I was born.

My girls, Makayla and Mallory, are for sure one of the greatest blessings I have ever received and to whom this book is dedicated.

Thank you to the many pastors in my life who helped me take a step each day closer to Jesus Christ with their messages. Growing up as a part of the Milroy United Methodist Church community of faith set the stage, but for sure my greatest understanding of my journey with Jesus Christ has come from my years as a member of White's Chapel United Methodist Church in Southlake, Texas, and Highland Park

United Methodist Church in Dallas, Texas.

Thank you to all the teachers who entered my life to get me a step forward in my education and life's journey. Thank you to the many mentors and coaches in my life, with special callouts to Paul J. Meyer and Tony Jeary.

Thank you to my siblings, my grandparents, and such an amazing extended family who were part of the village during my growth years and maturation into a functional adult. Thank you to my many bosses who taught me so much, from Ralph Richardi to Marilyn Devoe to Cornelius Boone and of course to the Camelot crew at DFW Airport. I will never forget what they taught me about life, relationships, and leadership.

Thank you to the Milroy Mafia crew who I grew up with and am still connected to today as if time never passed us by. Thank you to my broad circle of friends, business partners, and colleagues, many of whom I met during my incredibly blessed career at American Airlines. Thank you to the boys on the golf course each weekend who keep me grounded.

Thank you, God the Father and Jesus Christ the Son, who are the Light of my World and my path to redemption and salvation.

Foreword

Mark's book is a game changer!

The book you're about to read is going to change your life. It will have an impact on your thinking, your life, and your business, just like if you were to hang around the author, which I have for over a decade.

Mark lives a life that inspires. He's a giver and a thinker. Now as a gift to his two beautiful girls (Makayla and Mallory) and to you, he has given you these 17 Powerful Insights that will positively motivate your actions toward amazing results.

Ask yourself, Do I make a difference in the lives of others? Whether you answer yes or no, applying these principles will up your game. You will become a better you and over time take steps to become the BEST YOU.

Mark's LinkedIn bio is impressive, but what you see behind the scenes—the human he is—is even more inspiring. He and I have worked closely together personally and professionally for over a decade. At American Airlines I have been blessed to help Mark and his teams tackle many powerful assignments together, and time and time again I observed Mark lead those teams to execute and wow people. Beyond business, he is a passionate father who demonstrates love for his girls daily. His best days are spent with his wife, Gina, and with his girls.

Mark and Gina are both world travelers and adventurers.

Mark is a self-acknowledged sports junkie. He is passionate about serving others through his church, his community, and his company. He has been nationally recognized for actively serving his community for over two decades alongside organizations such as Junior Achievement, Kiwanis, Habitat for Humanity, and Relay for Life, a critical fund-raising organization for the cure for cancer.

When Mark decided to embark upon this project, I knew he'd be a light for others.

His aspirational epitaph, which I think provides insight into his identity and life purpose, is to be "a passionate disciple of Jesus Christ, who served others with humility and integrity and made a difference in the lives of others."

This book, *My Gift*, is about making a difference in the lives of others. When he started this book, the goal was for his girls, Makayla and Mallory, to benefit from his life lessons. Now, he wants to continue his life's mission of serving others by sharing these lessons with you. I know when you read and apply it, you will have the opportunity to become BEST YOU.

Mark has always been about faith and family first. He is a living example of filling life with experiences, not things. He has had a great deal of incredible business experience in airport operations, customer experience, and corporate roles. His current mission includes business transformation of shared services to American's People team, including HRIS SAP SuccessFactors digital transformation. He's spent years working with C-level executives, and his focus in leadership is to help guide individuals and organizations to increase effectiveness through Customer Experience, HR Business & Digital Transformation, Leadership Development & Coaching,

Organizational Change Management, Employee Engagement & Commitment Strategies, and Delivering Results. He's been serving others for decades and doing all those things for American Airlines. But look closer, and you'll find character traits we all wish we could live out every day. He is passionate about connecting people, building relationships, mentoring and coaching, driving strategic direction, delivering business transformation, and achieving results for others. This book and these 17 Insights will help you to become a better you, grow as a servant leader, and change your life.

TONY JEARY
The Results Guy™

Introduction

Life, Learnings, and Leadership

Life is a journey. It's full of stories, experiences, and of course, pain and joy. Each of us are on our own journey through life, and you've experienced many things too. You've had times of joy and other moments of frustration that you had to push through.

I feel like I am the richest person on earth, living the perfect life. To be clear, my bank account doesn't make me the richest, but I'm rich because I am blessed more than I deserve by having God's grace and His blessings in my life every minute of every day. I count my riches in faith, family, friends, opportunities, and experiences. And that perfect life? Well, I call it cognitive reframing.

I learned that my search for happiness and success came pretty much from the same place as Dorothy's did in *The Wizard of Oz*. Sometimes you must look "no farther than your own backyard" to find the answer. So, I often reframe my definition of happiness and success to be right where I am right now. And that's how I end up in that perfect place. I also realized that during that journey of life, we don't always end up where we think we wanted to be. In another movie, *The Sound of Music*, Maria says, "Every time God closes a door, He opens a window for us." He has done that for me too.

So now you also have some insight into my two favorite movies. I find that I have learned from movies, from music, from exercise, from travel, from so many places one doesn't always think that the learning will present itself to us. How about you? From where do you draw your wisdom and knowledge?

When I look back, I can see that I was fortunate and maybe a bit lucky to be very good at applying those when they came my way. As I matured, I realized how often God puts us (and we put ourselves) in places that don't seem ideal. Why?

When it happens, you may feel like the apostle Paul while in prison or like Daniel in the lion's den—maybe distraught at the circumstances but still hopeful that it's going to work out.

No matter what your adversity is, you must realize that during the event or in the situation at that moment, God has a much bigger picture than we do and a much bigger plan. It's up to us to step back and reflect to see what we can learn and how we can apply that to our life.

I began to think one day when I heard an amazing message in church from our pastor, Paul Rasmussen: "What if we truly believed He knew us in the womb" and "set us apart to do great things" as He did with others throughout the course of biblical history? Just think, what if we really believed that premise: How would it, how could it change our life?

It *has* changed mine, without question. I have learned a ton from the many great pastors in the churches where I spent time attending and as a member over many years. I have also been surrounded by some terrific coaches, teachers, leaders, bosses, and mentors in my life. Those came to me from family, friends, school, work, and more. I have highlighted some of those in this book with the intent to share a few things I was gifted with and learned from these people in my life.

These events can be the key moments of truth that give us wisdom, shaping us over the course of our lives. They can take us to a better place. They can be both personal and professional. We can grow as leaders from every experience as well: in our community, at work, and at home. I consider these events and moments "my gifts" from others.

I've held a variety of roles in my career as an executive with American Airlines. Leadership isn't just reserved for work of course, but I've been able to apply my growth and to my career in every role I've accepted. In my role as the leader of American Airlines' HR shared services practice, my team has been accountable for driving digital transformation, as well as leading transformation of the team and culture, at American.

When you think about that, this is foundationally relevant because American's leadership, since the merger of American and US Airways, has been keenly focused, as one of our top three corporate objectives, on building the right people-centered culture. Many of the things that we are doing are to help drive and set the foundation for what that looks like for the future of American Airlines.

Whoever you are as a leader is transferable to your kids and/or the people you mentor and lead. I try to teach my kids that you will experience a wide spectrum of people out there. People are going to do things to you whether you like it or not, and some things you're not going to like. Adversity is a very real part of life.

It's less about what happens to you. What matters is *how you respond*.

There have been times I've responded well and times,

like most people, when I could have responded better. How I responded to the divorce I was faced with, and how I responded to my kids, has impacted some of their decisions now as young adults. How I respond to adversity at work will impact outcomes and relationships long term. Overall, I think we got it right. But we're all still a work in progress.

How about you? How do you manage adversity when it comes, or when others do things to you that negatively or unfairly impact your life?

First, you've got to change your perception about the things that happen to you.

That's cognitive reframing.

It's how I think about life and how I hold a belief that true happiness comes from within. It doesn't come from external or material things. This may seem obvious, but it's worth focusing on and restating. We can get sidetracked. It's easy to forget what's most important.

I often tell people I'm living the perfect life, which also gets a funny response like, "Well, what do you mean?" I just reframed my definition of what a perfect life is to match where I am. Suddenly this new kind of happiness and joy comes out of me.

You too can develop that perspective about your life, about where you are, thereby changing how you think about things.

Whether you call it introspection or cognitive reframing, taking time to count your blessings can be amazingly uplifting right where you are, right now.

Many of these lessons and how you apply them to your life will be directly tied to your mindset and framing it for the right place. I think it's important to have the right mindset when you read a book that professes to have life lessons. My number one Strength Finder attribute is learning. I realized that about 20 years ago, and knowing that, I've tried to apply a life of learning, which has greatly impacted me in my life's journey. There's so much that people can benefit from if they simply think back and have the mindset to apply these they have been gifted with.

It is my hope that you can take away something from this book that positions you better in life with just one or more bits of wisdom to shape you into the person and the leader you want to become. By the way, I recognize we are all busy. So, if you want a glimpse into this book, you can go right to the end of each Insight and see the "Insights" and "Learnings" specific to that chapter and get an idea how they might be applicable to you too.

Thanks for taking this journey with me.

And thank you for taking time to read and to learn. I hope and pray that God's richest blessing will come your way as your journey continues.

Thank you again, Tammy Kling, Mark Nolan, Tiarra Tompkins, and the team at OnFire Books for helping me bring this book to life.

A Foundation of Faith

Learning from Others

This Insight highlights the lifelong benefits of learning.

I'm a lifelong learner. If you aren't familiar with personality tests, on Gallup's CliftonStrengths assessment (formerly known as the Clifton StrengthsFinder), my number one attribute is learning. I discovered that 20 years ago, and realizing that, I've tried to live a life of learning. I know that always being open to learning has greatly impacted me in my life's journey. There is so much that people can benefit from if they simply think and have the mindset to learn. When you have the right mindset, you can reframe things in your life and how you respond to events that occur to you.

There are so many moments in life that help us to become a better person. Good or bad, the moments that we experience create a collection of moments that create who you are. There are so many people I've had the privilege to learn from that I know have made me a better person.

During my first year at American Airlines, we had this guest speaker come in, and what he said impacted my life.

Very simply put, "Begin each day selecting terrific! It's your choice as to what you pick—so let's decide today to pick terrific! When you pass people in the hallways, when you wake up next to your spouse, it's up to you to decide how to start your day." It changed the way I started the day, and even now if you ask me, "How you doing?" I always try to respond with, "Terrific!"

Why does this make a difference in your day? Most people expect nothing other than, "I'm fine" or "It's good" or "Have a nice day." But when you say something like, "I'm terrific, it's outstanding," you get their attention! That speaker changed how I interact with people. It changed how I simply said, "Good morning" or "How are you doing?" or how I respond to those same greetings in a positive uplifting tone. It changes the interaction incredibly.

Jim Valvano, former coach at North Carolina State, talked about his cancer battle, trying to inspire others and give others the lessons he had learned. His speech was amazing! Coach Valvano says, "There's three things you want to do every day. You want to think, you want to laugh, and you want to cry." Think about how important it is to feel this range of emotions. I think about this, and I set aside time in my calendar to think, to laugh, and to cry. It is something that has changed how I lead, and how I act at work. If you've never heard this amazing speech, I encourage you to google it and experience it personally. Don't just take my word for it.

In all things, we will experience a wide spectrum of people in this world. When my children were younger, I tried to teach them that there are people who are going to do things to you; and some things you're not going to like. But it's less about what happens to you. What's important is how you respond.

We're all still a work in progress.

I call it cognitive reframing. Much of our lives and our own happiness, true happiness, that is, comes from within. It doesn't come from external things. How do you view your life?

If someone asked you about your life today and how you felt about it, what would be your response? I often tell people I'm living the perfect life, which always gets a funny response like, "Well, what do you mean?" The decision to have a perfect life is something every single one of us can choose. I chose to reframe my definition of what a perfect life is to match where I am. Suddenly this new kind of happiness and joy comes out of me. Your perspective about life, about where you are, whether it's introspection or cognitive reframing is so important. As you read this book, so many of these lessons and how you apply them to your life, will be directly tied to your mindset and framing it for the right place.

The three lessons Coach Valvano taught me—to think, to laugh, and to cry—will build your character and feed your soul. I know you might be thinking, *Why would I want to make time to cry?* It isn't about finding a reason to be sad.

What are you passionate about? You can be in your life working on something that you are so passionate about that it brings you to tears. I think about where and when to apply the passion in my life. I am a tough guy, but when I find myself thinking about situations I'm passionate about, it brings me to tears!

When I talk about Coach Valvano and the lessons that I learned from him, it makes me realize that throughout the many interactions in our life, there are so many missed opportunities to listen, to learn, and then apply it to our lives. The lesson in this is that you have a chance to learn from every person who comes into your life. Good or bad. Not just the CEO, but even getting to know the janitor. Everybody matters. Everybody at work or in your life plays a role in it and it matters. I encourage you to take advantage of every gift that comes your way.

Think back to how you start your day. As a leader, you have the opportunity to change the way people see something as routine as the question, "How are you?" The first way to do that is to model your life that way. "I'm doing terrific." Maybe you don't feel terrific. Let's be honest, we don't always *feel* terrific. Why say it if it isn't true? Because it is both inspiring and motivating. I've had moments where I don't feel terrific, but saying it to a colleague or a stranger, then seeing the look on their face and the difference in their day is something you can see. And it can change that less than terrific moment into something that is starting to closer resemble the truth.

Modeling behavior is the first step. The next step in that is to be willing to engage in conversation with people. Thirty plus years ago, this one guy has no idea that his orange-sized green sticker, which is now on my home office desk, and his speech about starting each day with terrific changed my life and that I never forgot to start my day that way.

Once you have gotten comfortable in your own life and modeling it, you can start to figure out how you can pass it on to your children, to your coworkers, to your friends,

One of the biggest lessons that I learned was when I was suddenly, at my own request, a manager of the passenger operations in the Dallas-Fort Worth airport. Every day I would walk the airport with my boss, and he wouldn't say much. To me, it felt like painful hours of walking when I had stuff to do, but I realized Jack was teaching me. He was walking with me and setting an example.

The biggest lesson that I learned from so many leaders throughout my career is that everybody matters. And by association relationships matter. It's all about relationships. We're in a people world, right?

Several years ago, the executive vice president of HR asked what kind of business we're in? The answers ranged from "airplane business" to "transportation business." My answer? "We're in the people business." Those moments in time with that Camelot crew, my first leadership group, taught me some of those most basic things. In one of those aha moments, I realized if I led by example and I made sure that relationships matter, I could instill trust and respect into those relationships. This became so valuable years later when I was leading our team in New York on September 11, 2001.

I had no idea what was going on, but I realized I was the only person in the city who had any idea what was going to happen next. I had a thousand people in an airport, all looking at me saying, "What's next? What do we do? What's going to happen to our jobs?"

It's those moments of inflection, those moments of truth where you can miss the opportunity, or you can seize the moment. And I realized in that moment that I was the person who had to make sure they knew it was going to be OK. That their jobs were OK. That my family was going through the same emotions as their families were. These are the moments where we grow—in the refiner's fire. Every single moment, every mentor, all of it up to that moment helped me be a leader in one of the toughest days in American history. I've built on all those lessons and share them as I mentor and teach people.

Key Takeaways and Insights #1

Learning from Others

• How does this lesson apply to you?

• What learning can you take away?

• Be aware that gifts of learning come your way every day.
• Never stop your learning.
• Sometimes you must cognitively reframe the event or the moment to get to a better place.
• True joy and happiness come from within.
• Take time daily to think and reflect so you take every opportunity to improve who you are and who you want to become.

A few lines from "May We All" by Florida-Georgia Line, who make the learning point well.

> *May we all do a little better than the first time*
> *Learn a little something from the worst times*
> *Get a little stronger from the hurt times.*

Trust the Process

*Trials can be the pivotal moments that form
some of our deepest faith.*

When I was four years old, I got really, really ill. My parents were taking care of the three of us: a five-year-old, a ten-month-old, and me. My getting sick took them off guard, as it does any parent, and we found ourselves in the emergency room with no idea what was wrong. The medical staff sent us to Riley Children's Hospital in Indianapolis to learn what was going on. I was diagnosed with what is now known as Wilms' tumor on my right kidney. Yes, I had cancer. At the time of that diagnosis, there was no known, prescribed cure. Only experimental treatment. My doctor, John P. Donahue, was the attending surgeon and medical professional. He explained everything to my parents, and they made the decision to go through that experimental treatment and surgery. Over the next several months and the next year or so I went through chemotherapy and other kinds of radiation treatments.

Talking with my parents years later, I learned it was their

faith and their family that got them through. I know the Lord was looking down on Dr. John Donahue when he cured me of that cancer. I wasn't cured all at once. It was treatment, surgery, more treatment, and more doctor visits. Dr. Donohue told my parents, "I didn't cure Mark, God did." During that surgery, I can literally right now close my eyes and picture my grandpa Hedrick handing me a watch as I was wheeled down a long hallway into surgery as a little four-year-old kid. I can still picture the hallway. I know the journey of cancer changed the faith that my family had, but it also influenced me during my life journey as well.

We always had a solid foundation of faith. My parents still attend the church that we grew up in. They have been members there since they moved to Milroy in 1961. The experience of faith has shown me not only how important it was for me to have faith and to be involved in church, but it also gave me a huge foundation of giving back. Everything that I saw my parents do when I was a kid, and even today, to give back to the church and the community, was part of creating a foundational belief that giving back is part of who you are in Christ. I know that the church was a huge part of my cancer journey as a kid. The friends and relationships that grew as a result of that cancer journey as young parents in need who had no idea what was coming next gave them a stronger faith. That church connection was there for them during the time of need, uncertainty, and hope when I was fighting cancer.

Without question, the best hope for this country, the hope of communities around the world, could be positively impacted by spending time in their local church.

When it comes to having a strong faith, it wasn't just a natural reaction either. When I was a child, I went to church because my parents took me—they made me go. As we grow older in our faith, and we get to make those decisions on our own, the choice to have faith, the choice to invest in time in a church is something that you must figure out. I didn't start going to church initially in college, but I did feel led to go back, and when I did, it felt like the right thing to do. Having faith is a decision.

Throughout the many years of learning and going to church, in 2007 during one of the harder times in my life, with my impending divorce, I realized I wasn't going to church because it felt right. It was because I needed God. I was devastated that my marriage was over. I needed that relationship with Christ, with God, because the marriage in which I promised "till death do us part" had failed. There was nothing on this planet that was going to give me the peace and the relationship that I needed more than God in those moments. I needed that relationship with my Creator. At that moment I knew this relationship was critical to my faith and that part of my life.

I know that my faith has impacted my girls as well. I have two daughters, Makayla and Mallory. At the time of the writing of this book, Mallory was twenty years old and Makayla was twenty-three. Each of your children are going to be different, and how they process their faith is never going to be the same. Their journey will be different, and you are just charged to walk beside them. Mallory, by her own choice during her freshman year in college, joined a local church, was baptized, and formally joined the church through confirmation as a young adult. That was her journey, and though her older sister was baptized as a small child, she is still trying to figure out her faith and what it means to and for her. I know it is inside her and the foundation is there as I see it in her character as a maturing young adult. She has a loving and giving heart. When you come to these pivotal moments with your children, it is important to give them space to be themselves and figure it out.

When I had that conversation with Makayla, I gave her my perspective and offered her the best wisdom that I could. Here's what I said: "You don't have to have proof, yet, that God exists. You'll figure it out over time or maybe you won't. What's the harm in believing? Because when you're in that moment in life, and you are in that foxhole, and you don't know what to do. If you're not a believer in God, you just keep looking and looking around for something to help you, right? If you're a believer, you have this thing called hope. You can say a prayer, you can ask for Christ Jesus, for this Holy Trinity that comes to intervene. You've got hope that the person on the other side of the foxhole doesn't have. So just think about in that moment, Which one do you want to be?"

My second example brought us to the Old Testament: "I knew you before you were in the womb. I set you apart to do great things" (see Jeremiah 1:5). Then I simply said to her, "What if you actually believed there was a God, and He picked you and put you on planet earth to do great things? How would you think differently about your life? What would you do differently if you believed you are here to do something great? 'Great' comes in various forms. In the Bible 'great' was defined by conquering nations. What would you do if you believed that?"

Do you know who you are? Do you know what you believe?

Several years ago, when I was trying to figure out who I was and who I wanted to be remembered as, I wrote my aspirational epitaph! This may seem morbid, but so many people don't consider that you can think about and plan how people will remember you. I wrote the things down that I hoped when I leave planet earth someday, that people will have written about me, or be willing to write about me. I really did those things in my life. It is an aspirational kind of epitaph. It says:

"He was a passionate disciple of Jesus Christ who served others with humility and integrity and made a difference in the lives of others."

That third point, "He made a difference in the lives of others," is also a bit of the inspiration, the legacy, the desire behind wanting to write this book—to leave something behind for my kids or any reader that picks it up over the next days, weeks, years, or decades.

When I typically say, "I've written my epitaph," people get a weird look on their face like, *Are you dying? What's going on here?* Rather it is the aspiration, the inspiration to pursue who I want to be on this planet.

It allows me to say no to some things in order to say yes to something better. Sometimes the right answer is, heck yes, like if I play golf Saturday morning, but sometimes it's like, "No, I'm not able to play golf because I committed to go build a Habitat for Humanity house with my church." I'm going to do something and make a difference for that family who gets a house. It allows me to say no to some things and say yes to something better and provides good framework to make different choices.

Faith is just part of one of many lessons you share with your kids. I had an opportunity to teach my daughter who, when it was time for college, didn't want to go quite yet. Makayla wanted to sit it out for a while and be a bartender to earn some money—in other words, take some time off to think and get a job. And I gave her a chance to do that. I helped her look at a budget if she were living on her own and if she were in college. Now college is important for other reasons beyond a degree, but I wanted it to be clear that on her own she is writing the checks, but if she went to college, I'd pay.

She made the decision to go to college, and although she has changed majors a few times, she called me during her next-to-last semester and said, "Dad, guess what? For the first time in my life, including high school and college, I got a 4.0!" In May 2019 I was privileged to watch her walk across the graduation stage with honors.

Through faith, through learning what to do and not do, everyone must have the opportunity to make their own choices. Each of your children will be different, and the people you meet and work with, they are all going to be different too.

The trials that I went through allowed me to choose a better path in my faith journey and truly understand why my relationship with God matters. It has shown me how, in that time of my life, God could be there for me. My prayer life became different, and now how I pray, how I worship has grown, and I know those moments of truth showed me to stay on the right path and continue building my relationship with God. It helped me see how I had built my relationships with those I love, and it showed me how I can practice my faith and have a willingness to be more open and share more. That is the biggest gift—"sharing your truth." The world needs you, and it needs me too.

Key Takeaways and Insights #2

Trust the Process

- How does this lesson apply to you?

- What learning can you take away?

- Trust the process; it is through both trials and tribulations that the gifts of learning come our way.
- Do you know your learning style?
- Your children are different—thus they learn differently and at a different pace. It is beneficial as we teach them to know how they learn.
- Faith is the foundation of my life and can be in yours too.
- Achievement of one's goals is often reduced to the level of one's habits. Successful people develop the new habits consistent with their goals. Are you prepared to "trust the process," applying what you learned during a difficult time, and to start those necessary new habits to achieve your goals?

Be a Humble Leader

Humility and service to others are two of the most
powerful leadership traits I've learned.

If I were to highlight one particular trait that will aid you the most in your career and life, it would be humility. Without humility, your life will be more difficult, and you will experience more instances of pain, embarrassment, and character tests. It's from a foundation of humility that most other critical human traits can be developed. These include gratitude, leadership, patience, and forgiveness.

Humility is a difficult trait to learn and practice.

It is exciting to me that I learned it from my parents. If I must pick one of them to put up on a pedestal momentarily, it would be my father. But I think both of my parents absolutely have exemplified humility. Their pictures could be in the dictionary in a couple of places. One of them would be next to the definition of *humility*, the other one being service. They have lived in the same house that they built for us since about 1972. My father and mother were both involved in the teaching profession. My mother was a schoolteacher, and my father was an administrator in the local school system. They always have been and still are involved in everything that matters in the community. When my father retired from being a school administrator, he became a pastor and today serves in the local church community and the local food pantry. The work continues.

Both my father and my mother exemplify the notion, the importance of living a selfless life. They were always focused on service to others and realizing that there are other things out there bigger than they. They always demonstrated that their own self-worth and self-importance are glorified by serving others. It's a life centered on humility.

Many people misunderstand humility and regard it as being meek or mild tempered. According to *Psychology Today,* some even characterize it as having low self-esteem or even acknowledging your personal lack of value. This couldn't be more to the contrary, because I have learned a humble person keeps their accomplishments, gifts, and talents in the proper perspective. They are consistently oriented toward others. My parents always valued the welfare and state of other people and have the ability to "forget themselves" and totally be about others in the room.

In his best-selling book *Good to Great,* Jim Collins found two consistent traits of CEOs in companies that transitioned from average to superior performance: humility and an insatiable will to advance the cause of the organization. This was confirmed in a recent survey of over 100 companies published in the *Journal of Management.* Humility in CEOs led to many important company top performance characteristics like higher-performing leadership teams, increased collaboration and cooperation, and flexibility in developing strategies.

At the same time, I learned it's important to be humble about one's accomplishments. This is more difficult than you might think. Why? Because when you work hard, you accomplish a difficult task, you should feel good about that. Humility isn't just hiding your accomplishments under a basket. It is being able to know you did a good job and not let it go to your head.

My parents are absolutely the model of where that comes through to my life. As a business leader, I have experienced many situations where arrogance was the norm. I watched people who knew everything—or thought they knew everything—work to make sure everyone in the room knew it. I realized whether I was or wasn't the smartest person in the room, I knew I certainly was not going to act like it!

Leaders don't look to be the smartest person in the room. They listen to others and build up their team so that they can cultivate new leaders. So, I began to listen. I began to take others' ideas into consideration. I read more. I began to realize that my own self-worth was more exemplified by being part of the team. I was best skilled at facilitating solutions rather than having to always come up with the "big idea." I discovered that I could accomplish more and have a bigger impact in the team-oriented approach than making all the calls myself. It really didn't surprise me that including everyone in the process was the best way of gaining their commitment toward implementation. People are more invested if they know that their opinion matters.

I can't think of the moment it clicked, but there was a moment during my career when I realized that you're not as smart as other people in the room. I don't know exactly when it was, but it was around the time when I came back from Los Angeles to take on the role of customer experience leader for American Airlines. My job was to create the new group and develop the strategy of customer experience for American's customers, internal and external.

My hiring manager, who at the time was the executive vice president and CMO for the company, said to me, "Here's what the role looks like. Here are all the pieces. You'll be a part of these 'think tanks.' You'll be driving strategy."

And I'm thinking, *Oh my God, I'm not that smart! Can I drive strategy? Can I actually do that part of the role?* The first part of accepting this new role was to admit that I wasn't the smartest guy in the room. Even though I wasn't, I cherished the thought of taking on this challenge. After all, it was a huge job and was a major opportunity to drive this pivotal strategy for the company. I was prepared for the challenge but had to acknowledge I would be the right choice for the job thanks to the value of my early lessons of humility and how it applied to my style of leadership. Yes, the company wanted me to lead the group, and I would be responsible for delivering the results, but it was how I led and the results of my track record they desired—not just me. The company was choosing me based on the potential I could bring in terms of leadership.

A long time ago I realized the team was more effective than any individual. And so, putting myself in that role of just being a part of that was enticing, and I was confident that I would do a great job. I clearly realized that my own self-importance was just a part of the bigger picture, just part of wheels God was orchestrating for me. I was also embarking on some major life changes.

It was during this same time I was going through my

divorce. I had moved back to Dallas from Los Angeles with my ex-wife (the mother of my children) and my two kids. At the same time, the light bulb clicked on for me about my faith and how much I needed that part to be in my life in a real way. It was this time of uncertainty of my marriage that my faith was a comfort. It was the solid rock that I would build everything new on. All these changes and challenges were converging together—the new job, the divorce, my relocation, changes for my children. Then I had an aha moment, this epiphany, this breakthrough: **Things were set up for this very moment and were orchestrated for me to reassess my life's approach.**

God and His Holy Spirit were making a move in my heart, causing me to self-reflect. What I once viewed as negatives in my life were really opportunities to change my life's thought approach and a chance to impact lives perhaps like I never would have again.

That's what I wanted! What I wanted and what I needed was a better approach to life. My spirit welled up in my chest, and I could only thank my God and Creator that He was with me and never left me even when I didn't deserve it.

Every day it becomes easier to see the life lessons from my parents, especially for the many examples of humility and its impact on others. Centrally it's a view of oneself that means there are other things more relevant, more important, and a higher calling that is just waiting for you to discover.

It ties back to the faith part of my life. Through his incarnation on earth, Christ humbled himself. He would later humble himself to take on all our sin and die on the cross. Our righteous Father, in human form on the cross, accepting God's will for His earthly body and dying, hung between two criminals, one hurling insults and the other crying out, recognizing God

Himself was by his side. Jesus answered him, "I tell you the truth, today you will be with me in paradise'" (see Luke 23:43).

We can learn from one of the two who were crucified next to Jesus. It is never too late to repent and ask the Lord to accept us. Jesus humbled himself to accept our sins, and we must humble ourselves to accept the hope of faith. Jesus cleansed this man from his sins, received him graciously, and justified him unconditionally. The same gift of eternal life is offered to us all.

Taking the approach of humility and sacrifice changes the way you think about things. I have friends who have gone through divorce like I have. And you know, there's many times there's a fight for the battle of the finances. I simply said, "Whatever is right for the mother of my children and for my children to position them for success." I think the split was something like 85/15. I just said, "I'll figure it out." I had faith; I knew no matter what the outcome that I was a child of the King, and he would never leave me destitute. I can only say that it was a major moment of humility that God Himself was at work in my life. I said to myself, *I'm going to be just fine—now and forever.*

All I can say was a "shift happened" in the way I thought about events and the way I began to see life. As my new boss recapped for me all the things I would be responsible for, the level of control I would have, and the role I would play, an inner voice whispered, *I can do that. You can do that.* I remained calm but felt like jumping on the chair like Tom Cruise on *The Oprah Show*! I listened, and then I thought, *I am perfect for this job.* I stopped listening to the sales pitch during the conversation and the small talk in the room. It got to the part of the conversation where I had to respond with some meaningful, pivotal statements that would make or break my moment. My head swirled with thoughts. *What if I want to be good?... I can't be just good because I'm great at it already.* Before I responded, a different approach was heard. It suddenly became, **"I can do all things through Christ who strengthens me"** (Philippians 4:13 NKJV).

Maybe not word for word, but in spirit and attitude that verse rang over and over in my mind, changing the view of my own perspective and what I brought to the table and valuing the role of others. Thank you, Mom and Dad; thank you, Jesus!

Over the next four years, my life bubbled over from that view of myself, the realities of my approach, and the trajectory I have been enjoying from that moment on. From a company contribution view, there are initiatives that we put in place in 2007–2008 and are still in place today. During my time in that position, I loved the outcomes that my teams achieved.

Today at American we have the Customer Cup. We created the Customer Cup to build competition between airport teams who are focused on delivering an improved customer experience. The award recognizes airport teams for their performance in serving customers at the airport across five primary customer touch points. Those touchpoints are departure dependability, turn flight dependability, baggage performance, customer feedback, and overall airport satisfaction. The Cup idea was birthed through a team approach. It was a result of generating ideas from a diverse group of employees.

The Customer Cup is part of a broader focus the airline has put toward improving the experience for its customers. With more than 250 employee teams across the network during my time in the role, American encourages all employees to bring forward ideas and solutions to problems they've identified in the travel experience. Airports across the network compete for the Customer Cup honor quarterly. All employees contribute and can earn network bragging rights and even enjoy a party in their honor for working hard to improve the airline's customer service rankings. It has created a life of its own and generates marked and continuous improvement across the organization. Winning the company's coveted Customer Cup for the first time is an extraordinary tribute to the hard work and dedication of each employee—and it's a lot of fun!

The team approach and encouraging employee participation really are built on the value of humility, which really drives better and bigger results far better than I ever could have done on my own.

And that's just the beginning. I had to recognize that my role at the time was the leader. I was the ultimate decision maker if we needed to make decisions or break ties. I know that had I not taken it from the team approach, I would have probably driven decisions that were suboptimal, invalid, and potentially not the most effective. It would have reflected poorly, as the results of the team, the company wouldn't have been as great, and we wouldn't have seen the level of success that the team produced.

Last spring, we were conducting performance reviews for closing out the year and starting the new quarter at American with its goals and goal setting. In the same time frame, I had held an all-hands with my team of about a hundred, where I talked about these amazing results we achieved. I shared the results with the team, making sure they understood that some of what was achieved was truly remarkable. I told them, "Give yourselves a round of applause!" so they would really know what a great improvement that was from what we had done during that previous year.

Less than a week later, we're talking about those achievements in response to performance reviews. Not only would I be reviewing my managers, but they would be doing the performance reviews of their direct reports. I had to ask myself, *What category do I put them in for performance reviews? Are they in a good place? Are they in a great place?* Why was I asking myself amidst the celebration of our achievements? Because even if the team wins, it doesn't mean that members of that team don't need improvement.

I had to remind managers that just because we achieved great results does not mean that everybody gets a great rating. Those results were a direct correlation to good people working together to create synergies and proof that when you bring together multiple people, you can achieve great results. I reminded them to think about that. Not everyone's going to be a 10 on a scale of 10. When you're rating people, you can't base your review on the power of the many when you know it outweighs the power of the one.

I've also had some experiences reporting to a boss or a boss's boss who thought they knew more than anybody else. I learned then what not to do.

Humility is a muscle. Use it or lose it. You've got to work it, and you always have to keep in mind that it's never perfect. At times we're going to make mistakes. One of the first keys to keeping your humility muscle strong is by practicing active listening. No matter what you do or where you lead, humility starts with being a good listener—regardless of the topic of conversation that's going on at the time or if it's a personal decision you're about to make in your life. If you're willing to invite others to the conversation—your spouse, your kids, your coworkers, your boss—and you're willing to toss out a question or an open-ended topic, then you are making the decision to invite their feedback. Be a good listener!

Inviting others to the conversation on the topic at hand starts with your decision. Once they engage, you must behave in a way that demonstrates what active listening is all about. It must be more than just a stunt or gimmick. Make sure you truly digest the opinions of others in an inclusive, collaborative environment.

If you do this, one of three scenarios are likely to happen:

First, either you will be affirmed through the conversation that the direction you are on was the right one.

Second, you might conclude from feedback and experience drawn from many that it was the wrong one.

Third, if I engage in aggregate conversation, I might just get to a better solution. I might just get to a better answer than what I came up with and would have ultimately wasted a lot of time trying to pursue.

The net result of the process is pretty good too. So for me, inclusive, collaborative team dynamics is too positive to pass up. Active listening and being engaged with your team is my strength. I wasn't the smartest guy in the room. You must admit it.

Today I really don't dissect it like that anymore. It's been my style from continued use over and over. Like a habit, it's just listen and learn. Just like Mom and Dad always stressed, and are great examples of, taking the approach of humility and learning is the absolute principle that comes out of that. You get smarter and look smarter.

Interestingly, there is a lot of research on humility that shows that this trait has great value in the corporation. So much so that today's HR companies will try to assess humility in candidates. It's easier to assess than you think with all the access to social media sites. Look through someone's Facebook and you can see if they are probably humble or self-centered. Humility is a predictor of several other important life indicators. Acts of being humble have been linked with better academic performance for a long time. There is an absolute connection with better job performance and even evidence that humble leaders make excellent CEOs and leaders of organizations. Like my parents, humble people have better social skills and are more people centric. Humility hardly ever produces misinterpreted relationships and complexity in social interaction. Humble people tend to be genuine in all their social dealings and consistently are found to be more forgiving, grateful, and cooperative. Sound like a good leader?

Making a connection between humility and generosity is not difficult. People who are humble tend to be more generous with their time, their talents, and their money. So not only is humility that one trait desirable as a CEO for a successful organization, it is desirable for today's productive society. It's a trait of some of the most valuable members of society. You see it every day on the news. World changers are often humble of heart and generous with their gifts and talents.

As my oldest daughter, Makayla, was finishing high school, she was very adamant that she didn't want to go to college right away. As any child's parent, you want to step in and help them decide what's best, heavily leaning on your ideas, of course. I didn't think that was such a good idea. I also knew, from experience, that no one who pushes their ideas and agenda will ever be truly heard. I had to listen and learn and listen and learn to what she was saying to me to figure out how to help her get to a better place. Through that exchange, we both learned a lot, and thankfully she went to college, and she has graduated this past summer. She's even talking about going to graduate school. If I hadn't been a good listener and didn't realize, this isn't about me, it's about her, I wouldn't be able to help her make the right decision. After all, it's her decision. Now, I could have demanded that she go to college. I could pound my hand on the table and say, "You're going to college, and you're going to get good grades. You're going to study, and you're going to live here!" Sound familiar? But I realized it had to be her choice.

Active listening works and the principle outcomes and results are enhanced. It works as a parent and as a leader. If you want to see positive results, you must be willing to take a different approach.

Commitment to Faith

I am grateful for having a family committed to their faith early in my life. Each week, willingly or unwilling, they would take me to church and invited me to do the things to grow in my faith from confirmation, to youth fellowship, to baptism, to whatever it was. Humility was discovered at an early age, especially when I tied it back to the things I learned in my life around one's faith.

"For God so loved the world that he gave his one and only Son, that whoever believes in him shall not perish but have eternal life" (John 3:16).

Think about the last supper and how Jesus Christ humbled himself into the form of a servant to wash the feet of the disciples. This was Christ's example of being a humble servant to perform that act. Why did that matter to Christ? Because humility and being a servant to those around you were critical traits then and still are today. Jesus showed these perspectives by allowing them to be recorded in the Bible as example of how Jesus did earthly life, then gave them to us as an important example of how I should be modeling my life!

It's a faith story that my parents introduced to me during my childhood life. I mentioned earlier that my parents were involved in everything in the community and are now eighty-two and eighty. Their phone rings when I'm there. And eight out of ten times, I promise you it's someone asking for advice or help from them because they know they're always there. This behavior of helping others, serving others, and humbling yourself into the service role are the lessons I learned from my parents, and they will be forever valuable.

I am reminded of a sermon I heard several years ago. The pastor asked, "Do you believe you are here for a purpose, and if so, can you believe that there is a God and He gave you that purpose?" It made me stop and think for a second, and as someone who grew up around faith, the answer for me is clear. I try to think about someone who may be just starting their faith journey. What are their thoughts? *Is there actually a God? What if there is a God, and He is that big and all-powerful, all-knowing, and He's full of grace.* Tall order in this disenfranchised world. For me, I believe, and it is humbling to think about the presence of a God and what He's created and what He has done for me. It just reminds you of who you are and where you are. It brings you back to your melody and reminds you that it's bigger than you.

If you want it to be a part of your life, then ask for it. And how simple is that, right? How big is that. And how small I am. To me its mind-blowing. But I believe I was put here for a purpose. I don't know what that purpose is exactly yet. I believe it is still evolving.

A decade or so ago as previously stated, I wrote my own epitaph. It may sound morbid to you, but it created the aspirational life purpose that I seek to achieve every day. Then it manifests itself in my spouse and my kids and my friends and my work and this book. I do want to be that better Mark. I heard a sermon as I was writing this chapter in which the preacher said, "Joy is the predetermined choice to praise God no matter what." Wow! That is a powerful statement. No matter what's going on in my life, how complicated or challenging, praise God, give all glory to God. As the service continued, he laid out several points. First, that with inner joy comes true happiness. Second, that joy comes when we believe we're all made with a purpose. Why are we here? Third, joy comes when we are believing God will work things out. No matter what I am believing, God's not done with me yet. I can take a moment and learn about the situation at hand and figure out where it's going with His guidance. Lastly, joy comes when we choose it.

Joy is a choice. Joy is not a feeling. Joy is an active verb about choosing to have a lifestyle that lets you shine God's light. It is bigger than me. I am a humble servant of Christ Jesus when I should continue to form my life in a way that makes me choose joy. There's God! He's the Almighty, who will help me shape the outcome and help me get through whatever life brings my way.

When you choose a life of faith, it can be your purpose. It can help you drive the purpose. And when you're willing to sit back and realize that your God is not done with you yet, then you're willing to learn.

Mentors

I have been blessed to have people who have mentored me both at and out of work. Early in my career, a relative, Paul Meyer, took an interest in me at every family gathering to talk about his work and share with me things that he could teach me. I adopted Paul as a mentor for a decade or more. More recently Tony Jeary has become an incredible executive coach, personal coach, and life coach. He has taught me so much. A leader named Ralph Richardi was my first vice president where I was a direct report to a vice president. Ralph was the consummate servant leader, coach, and team builder.

In any company and in any role, anyone can instill leadership wisdom. Don't limit yourself to thinking only the CEO can teach you something. The janitors are as important as the CEO in our approach to people and relationships. That was one of the many lessons that Ralph taught me. It wasn't just his words; he taught me things through his daily actions and behaviors. And I know he was consciously doing this, but it subconsciously was influencing me as well. I couldn't help but watch what he did, how he talked, how he built the team, and how he treated people and responded to people. I've been blessed.

Another terrific mentor was Marilyn Devoe. She gave me autonomy and empowered me to run the business. The common theme among the four of my mentors would be relationships: Paul's and Tony's teaching, executive, and organizational coaching. Marilyn and Ralph have that common thread of "people matter" woven throughout their teachings.

When I left Dallas, I went to New York to oversee American's operations in LaGuardia airport just before September 11, 2001. It was that early-2000s time frame that Ralph came to New York to visit. When he came to the city, we took a walk through the terminal then headed down to have lunch. After several minutes he looked at me and said, "You're the mayor."

I kinda laughed and asked, "What do you mean?"

"You know everybody," he said. "You know the port authority police, you know the shoeshine guy, you know the guys that run the restaurants, and your gate agents know you."

It was something I had learned from him. He was the mayor of DFW because he understood it is important to build relationships, make people feel important, make them feel valued, and included. Great things could be accomplished. It doesn't matter if it's a sky cap or a gate agent or the restaurant guy; they're all going to help you be successful.

Almost daily I would go to the ramp team's break room and say hi to the guys on the ramp who are responsible for the baggage handling elements. I would say good morning to the skycaps and to anyone I saw.

Pretty soon the guys on the ramp invited me to play softball with them. Before you knew it, they started to joke about me being the only management guy on the team. So I replied, "I know that you know that I can play softball. And the only reason why I'm on the team is because I can hit it a softball." It changed our relationship! The work stuff got easier because they saw me get dirty, drink a beer, and hit a softball on the field. It changed our whole relationship at work, and it made us more successful together. I knew I was the boss, but why would I make all the decisions if I could get better results by asking people at the airport what their thoughts were? What did I find? Their ideas were pretty darn good.

When you're the "mayor," people ask you every day, "How do I do this? What do I do in this situation?" My first question back was, "What do you think you should to do?" They would pause and tell me their thoughts, and most of the time, it was a great idea. Asking gave me the chance to learn from them, and they felt empowered. The result? Better customer experiences. I realized my opinion may not be the best because I lacked the experience as a new manager. So I said, "Let me listen and learn." Sometimes you just get lucky. I had some good mentors that gave me some good advice, and I took it.

Key Takeaways and Insights #3

Be a Humble Leader

- How does this lesson apply to you?

- What learning can you take away?

- Humility matters; it really builds your character.

- Mentors matter. Surround yourself with people to teach you things that matter and fill your blind spots. (We all have them!)

- Everyone matters—from the janitor to the CEO. Build strong relationships. Make everyone feel valued.

- Serving others is a key point to humility. Find a way and place to give back your time, talent, and resources.

Redemption Is Attainable

This Insight offers that redemption is attainable,
and it's never too late.

People can change, and God can redeem. This is one of the pivotal things a person can learn about who they are. This isn't about "who you are" when no one is looking. This is who you are when the only one who can see inside you is God. It's who are you at the core, what are your values, and what do you stand for?

Not even necessarily just who we are in Christ, but how through our affirmation of faith, we form our life goals and then how, throughout life, those change and evolve. Even how we see ourselves in Christ changes.

There are many people with faith of all ages who have never thought much about it. For me, during my last two years at American Airlines, the company has been going through a reinvention or rediscovery of what kind of company we wanted to be. As the leader focused on training and leadership development, I have been championing the team to determine our purpose.

These are the same questions you must ask yourself. What's your purpose? What drives you? The first time American did this session, I met all kinds of people from all walks of life who were prepared to have this introspective reflection. I'm blessed, because I already know my purpose and I've known it for years. It can really change how we think about ourselves. In my case, it's an aspiration. It's who I want to be. I want to be the better me.

As our company's annual leadership conference came up, the biggest theme of the conference was, "Who is American and what is our mission statement? How do we connect to that purpose?" It was a series of working sessions and activities. It's fascinating to listen to other people who are having these "who am I?" moments. *What's my purpose? What's the better me? Or, Who am I today?* It was fascinating to see where different people are in their life with that question. It is instrumental to becoming a better person, a better you, which of course is the theme and goal of this book. I'm grateful to have great coaches and terrific people who gave me good examples to shape my beliefs. Our life experiences and the people who invest in us do, in fact, shape our beliefs.

Those beliefs determine the actions that we take and the results that we get. If I don't like what I'm getting, I ask myself, *How do I change it?* Why? Because experiences have shaped what and why we believe that. If I want to change their belief on my own, I've got to create new experiences to have them feel like it's a different and better path. It's one of the reasons why people change—because the situation or place you offer them is better than where they are today. But they make the decision. It's how you approach the work. It is so fundamental to the way I think these days. When I think about me and who I became, have become, and am still becoming, I am who I am today because of the foundation I had as a very young age with my parents.

I grew up in rural Indiana. I'm the son of a schoolteacher and school administrator and ultimately the son of a pastor. But all that influence, and the fact that I grew up on a farm, has given me a work ethic that is hard to come by. From farms to factories, those jobs and experiences shaped the work ethic that I have today as a fiftys-something adult. Many of the experiences shaped much of who I am. The importance of attending church was instilled in me by my parents, and because of that I've grown in my faith over the years by going to church and learning from pastors and growing through the church experience.

We grew up with real manners. We said please and thank you. We were respectful to others. We opened the door for people, and we didn't eat until everyone was served. My experiences shaped a foundation of traits and beliefs that I have relied on in life. I am so grateful for them. If I had to grow up again, I would want the same type of experiences.

Does that mean that I want to live an identical life to the one I had as a child? No way! I may have grown up in Indiana on a farm, but I don't want to live there now. I enjoy the big city of Dallas, I like traveling the world, and I love what those experiences have given me. While our foundation is laid at an early age, and no matter who we are, or what's shaped us as teenagers, those experiences will be brought forward into who you are as a young adult and ultimately as a grown adult. In the midst of this learning and shaping, you have a choice.

Through that process, if you're not continually learning, you will never get to that better place.

Allowing Others to Challenge Your Thinking

Years ago, I met someone on an airplane who challenged some of my thinking. While I didn't know the importance of that meeting until hours later, I knew he was there for a purpose. And through that time together, he helped me get clarity about some important issues in my life at that time. Later, when I contacted him for some more discussion, in one of our first meetings, he took out these index cards and asked me to write down my values. Have you ever stopped to think what your values are? When I stopped to really think about them, it gave me pause. It made me really think.

Mark's Core Values:

Faith, Attitude, Honesty, Humility, Freedom, Respect, Inspiration, Philanthropy, Wisdom, Effectiveness

Learning comes from engaging with others. Now, I love to debate. Some might call it argue. Even if I agree with the person who I'm studying with, I might take an alternate view of the debate because one of a couple of scenarios can happen. Either we have a conversation that helps me learn and can lead me to a better perspective, or I might learn information that reaffirms my previous perspective. On many occasions I have gotten totally new information and walked away thinking something very different.

That's why inclusion and diversity matter in this. If we continue to surround ourselves with people just like us, there really isn't much opportunity to debate, discuss, or even learn. Inclusion and diversity in the corporate world are critical, especially when you're operating a global company. You must be inclusive of people of all faiths, of all sexual orientations, of all ethnic backgrounds. It matters that we bring new experiences to the table, to be more tolerant and understanding and to find ways to be more understanding and inclusive. It enables us to get to a better place by having those conversations and those work experiences. We run a better business as a result.

Instilled Values

Just before I went off to college, my parents didn't really have a curfew for me. Even though I was still in high school, the only requirement was that when I got home, I said, "Hey, Mom, I'm home." They trusted me. I felt a huge respect for that. If it was a Saturday, no matter how late I came in, the next day we would get up and get ready for church. This was foundational and important because as I grew through adulthood, the care and concern my parents showed for me and my spiritual well-being stayed with me. It created an incredible respect for my parents.

As any college student would say, the easiest thing to do was to go out on a Saturday night with the gang and sleep in Sunday morning. Isn't that what college kids do? But something inside me during my freshman year said, "I'm different." I knew that I needed to be different, because in my heart this church thing still mattered. I knew it was the right thing to do. I mentioned it to other people at school that I wanted to get together a group of anyone who wanted to come with me. Some students really didn't really care about going to church, but several did, and we all started spending our Sunday mornings in church.

It felt relevant to me. As a child I went to church because my parents made me. As a college kid, I went because it felt like the right thing to do. Something was missing when I didn't attend on Sundays. The connection and the fellowship mattered to my daily walk. "Where two or more are gathered…"

It is during crisis and tragedy when we truly learn to lean on God. That time happened for me during my divorce in 2007–2008; those were powerful moments that made me realize how much I needed it.

I realize that without that experience, without my heavenly Father to help me work through events, or without a place where I could dump my burdens, I couldn't figure it out myself, and I would have been lost. When I was buried in the Word and dedicated to my faith was when things started to change for me. Even amid that painful situation, I had a great peace and clarity about myself.

I found a way to be a good father to my kids in divorce. I don't know if I would have been there without the foundation my parents gave me.

The Strength in My Faith and Love without Judgment

I recently had a lunch conversation with a colleague, and she looked at me and said, "Does it bother you that [friend one and two] don't go to church and don't believe in God?" As a Christian who lives out loud, I often find people ready to hear where I stand on all manner of topics.

"Whoa, that's a powerful question," I replied. "I wonder what those people do in times of need and struggle. I wish I could share with them and convince them how much Jesus has done for me." And of course, I have tried, but I wish I could share with them to convince them how powerful that relationship is for me personally and how much God wants the same for them.

I think that's the most powerful way we can share it. I believe it's best to explain how God has worked in your life and let them know in a personal way that it impacted you. It's important to let them know how God has moved in your life and then let God work on their hearts. Plant the seed. If you look at the church from the perspective of the skeptic, it can look like a large community that is exclusive, catering to only those with the secret passcode.

In reality this is just a type of isolation created and planned for by the enemy, Satan. The idea of divide and conquer has been an effective spiritual and worldly strategy forever. But for some, the idea of a church setting may not be attractive, and it can be very disenfranchising for people who haven't had any kind of personal faith experience or have had a previous bad experience in a faith-based organization. But if they went out of their way to experience it once, they likely want to be part of it. Hopefully each one of us would pursue other ways of connecting to a church or church leader for spiritual support. Today there are so many online opportunities to connect and hear a great message.

One Sunday morning I went to church, and that was on the heels of the previous week when the United Methodist Church reaffirmed their church doctrine that a member of the LGBTQ community could not be a pastor in a Methodist church. They also affirmed their position on not having same-sex marriages conducted in the church. When I read the news midweek, I realized they got it wrong. Now, I'm a member of the United Methodist Church. I have been for decades. How could the church get this wrong? I love my church, but this time they were wrong.

The next week I went to church Sunday morning, and our pastor delivers a great message in which he states, "Sometimes the big church gets it wrong. The governing body, the big organization, gets it wrong." He goes on and clarifies, "Yes, I'm bound as a pastor to follow the doctrine, but at this church in Highland Park, we were yesterday, and we are today, a church that welcomes everybody. All people are welcome in this church. It is Christ's table, not ours, and all are welcome." As our pastoral leader, he reminded us, and I think he probably reminded the Methodist Church last week too, that Jesus Christ called us to a new commandment:

"A new command I give you: Love one another. As I have loved you, so you must love one another" (John 13:34).

Called to Love

I loved the way that our pastor brought the message back to life and to the local church to redefine who we are and how we manifest our faithful positions and our biblical positions to views of love. I know our heavenly Father was proud of us that day. *WWJD* (What Would Jesus Do?) could never have a more profound application!

How we respond to things like this determines who we are as a people and what kind of relationships we have. It's been a difficult issue, and everyone's been talking about the church being divided. I know some pastors in the church who are excited and affirmed the church's position. But there are a lot of pastors and lay people in the church who are scratching their heads, saying, "How's that possible?" Nobody in this world escapes adversity. Everyone must deal with adversity, and now we had adversity right in front of us in the church. Jesus summed it up best in the book of John.

> "I have told you these things, so that in me you may have peace. In this world you will have trouble. But take heart! I have overcome the world." (John 16:33)

We are victorious. We can have peace in that.

Today I try to avoid the news because it seems to be one of those things where finding something uplifting is so rare. The Bible says that you need to "guard your heart" (Proverbs 4:2). Personally, I will admit how terrible things can be, and I will go overboard on how I know we can do better. It's why Jesus died for us—to reclaim us back as God's children because we never could make it on our own. It's so relevant and will remain relevant, because this has been a struggle with the world and church forever.

Your Faith, Your Choice

It can be very discouraging knowing that so many people today give their identity over to a governing body of the church. They bury themselves in the rules that are created by a giant governing body and forget that they have already been given an instruction guide they can trust (the Bible). What they should consider doing is to sit down with their Bible and see what God Himself says about such things and figure it out for themselves. Your church is there to supplement your walk; you are meant to feed yourself on God's Word. The pastor talks about the Bible and our faith. He talks about how you can't just become a good Christian or disciple of Jesus Christ without doing four things.

He states that people who look at the Bible and practice their faith purely strictly on Scripture probably don't see the big picture. There are other people who simply try to think their way through it. Most things are complicated and are real challenges for those two groups. Our pastor said if you take these four things and put them together, you will most likely have the best chance to see your path forward and be a faithful Christian.

1. You should read the Scriptures. I absolutely read the Bible and read about it.

2. You should also use reason. It's good to think about it, discuss it, debate it, and understand the context. Look up word translations; so much is different from the old language to the new.

3. You should be a part of the traditions of the church. You should go to communion. You should go through baptism. You should do these kinds of things, and you shouldn't just live it for yourself. These symbols matter.

4. Be part of a community of faith and experience what being a member of a local church is all about. Be part of the love and the change Christ called you to be part of. This is when you can really see what the body of Christ is all about.

You can do any one of these things and try to feel fulfilled in your faith. Without all of them, you will just find it difficult to make sense for what is wrong in the world.

It is easy to blame a church full of people for the things wrong in the world. The Bible is full of obscure verses. Someone who hasn't done their research or spent time in the

Word can try to take a story or part of a story out of context
to draw a conclusion or provide a less than informed perspective. It's like taking something from the Old Testament, which
was then updated by the New Testament, without any context
of when or why it was included in the written Word of God.
Most people I have met who belong to a mature community
of believers and work through issues and crisis together using
the God's Word as their guide seem to do all right. I read
Scripture daily, and I try to practice every part of the tradition.
It isn't legalism to follow tradition. Each act gives me a chance
to participate and worship in a way I feel glorifies God.

I go to service weekly, and I go to communion. I really
love the church and all it does. I am a part of a local church
who actively participates in Habitat for Humanity and in
Carpenters for Christ. Carpenters for Christ provides eco-
nomical and affordable housing in the local community.
Think back to all four of the pastor's tenants concerning your
faith journey. If you join the body of Christ, then it is your
responsibility to be active in your Christian education. It also
provides some structure that will help people get the idea of
Christianity or religion right. It's helpful to study the Bible in
groups to fully understand the Bible in a historical context
by thinking about it, experiencing its history, and working
through issues in your work life. You can't do it through a single lens. No one is perfect, and things happen in our lives that
we can't explain. People have blind spots that impact how they
comprehend situations. If you ever take just the Bible and read
it, your interpretation is impacted by your blind spots. That's
not a bad thing—everyone has them—but sometimes they
really can distort the truth. But if you take the Bible, plus tradition, plus reason, plus experience, plus study, and combine

them with being part of a local body of like-minded believers, your blind spots start to go away.

These experiences, mashed together, are how we become who we are. As we mature, we can change when we are willing to break down our blind spots, acknowledge them, and then learn from others and include others in the conversation.

Faith, the Church, and Socialism

People seem to get faith and the concept of the church as reason or example for socialism. Socialism, by definition, is a very economic-driven policy. And that's not in the context by which Christ took on the will of the Father. Jesus surrounded himself with lepers, sinners, and tax collectors. He wasn't sitting at a table of the top leaders in the community.

If you think about inclusion and diversity, Christ's surrounded himself with all different types of people. Christ was inclusive and wanted to save everyone He met. Including me and you. He wanted to make sure people knew of God's grace. This was aimed and exalted at the poor, not just the rich and the wealthy, who are already seemingly blessed in life. The path Jesus provides us is open to everyone. Oh, Christ wasn't modeling socialism. Christ was modeling inclusion and diversity at its finest level 2,000 years ago. I can only shake my head when a politician says something like, "Your Savior, Jesus Christ, modeled socialism." I shake my head and say, "No, Jesus modeled inclusion and diversity better than anybody." He asked us to love our neighbor as ourselves.

These are important issues. It's good and healthy to struggle with some of them, but to really be all you can be, to be the best you, your faith must be a priority. Your relationship with your Creator must be at the top of your list of important values to cultivate. I guarantee that when the time comes, and you get to see the entirety of your life, you will agree. It's never too late. You are shaping who you are when you make the same decision I did in college: I felt like church was important, it was necessary, and I wanted it to be part of my life. As a young adult I didn't know what my principles and affirmations of faith were. Are you shaping those principles based on who you are in Christ? Are you shaping those based on who you are in the church? Or are you just discovering? Wherever you are, there's no wrong answer. God wants to take you right where you are and light your path to your purpose.

Who Are You?

Has anyone ever asked you this? It was interesting when I was asked to write down my "why" or who I am. It came very easy to me at the time. It wasn't like I'd never thought of this before. My life experiences, my teachers, and the gifts I've received from others—that wisdom and other life lessons I accumulated right then. Success is different for everybody, but to me, success is right where I am right now. Today! I'm in the best place I can be. If I want to go someplace else, that's great, but I'm good—I'm really good—with who I am and where I am. I defined success as being the best Mark at this very moment. I'm the best Mark. And am I moving in that direction to be the better Mark in my health and in my faith as a parent, as a brother, as an uncle, as a leader at work. It's not trying to be richer than Bill Gates. It's about being the best Mark can be in the life that I have right now. If I achieve that, I will have more praise to offer, and I will know I was extended grace upon grace which gave me a great life.

While I wouldn't mind having some of his money, I wouldn't

want to be Bill Gates. Gates doesn't have two kids named Makayla and Mallory. He's not married to Gina. That's who I am. That's my why and who I want to be. I want to be that person. Purpose matters!

Even if I wanted to be, it's highly unlikely that I could be the next Larry Bird or Magic Johnson. I'm not that tall, nor can I dunk a basketball at six foot one and fiftys-something years old. I wouldn't mind having a jump shot like Larry Bird, but I'd rather focus on trying to be the best Mark possible. That's where I think you find that true joy that the Bible talks about. It's a predetermined choice to praise God no matter what. Wherever I am, whatever situation I face, I should praise Him for who I am and the opportunity He's given me. With that mindset, you can experience real joy in your life.

What Is Adversity?

It's when we have all those "hard time" moments. The question is, Will you be able to overcome them easily?

I feel confident in who I am and how far I have come in the decisions I've made. I always have this level of confidence and joy, knowing that God has greater times ahead for me. I always am careful to not miss the moments when everything gets hard and we really don't understand what's happening. I'm not perfect; my response isn't always grace and gladness. But I have assurance that He has me in that place for a purpose. I may not realize it's just a learning moment that is preparing me for something bigger in the future. Or, God's purpose could be for me to meet someone else and help them along. Sometimes (most of the time), it's not about me.

We must go back to the most core beliefs that we were made with a purpose. God knew you in the womb and set you apart so that you could do great things (see Jeremiah 1:5).

When we have those times where it's rough—like my bank account was hit, or I'm getting a divorce—it's difficult to see that you were made for great things. But the truth is, you really do have to go back and realize that God made each of us with a purpose. I believe that! I also believe that all things are possible in Christ. If I believe what God has told me as the truth, then that means he's not done with me yet. My job right now, in those low points, is to keep learning while he's working me through this—this thing, this event, this experience right now. And choosing, while I'm there in those moments, to be the best Mark possible.

It's almost always during the highs and the low that we want to put God aside. When things are challenging or trying, we try only to figure things out by ourselves. That is the wrong way! We find fault in someone else or lay blame versus taking responsibility and be accountable. When things go well, we want to take all the credit. In reality, God allows us to be weakened so that we can lean on Him. It's during these times that we reveal who we are more than anything.

Do I run into hiding from God? Or do I seek God further?

If you're going to hold to and really believe that we were made with a purpose, that believing all things are possible in Christ and God will help us with those things, that joy comes quickly and your faith will grow exponentially. Do you know what else grows? Success! You have reached a plane, and honestly, it is harder to be a better you because you're in your inner joy. Your inner peace has achieved a level that just can't get much higher.

What Do You Pray For?

When I was younger, I used to pray for stuff. Stuff is easy. I used to pray for very specific things, then waited for God to meet the desires of my heart. Years later I realized it was worthless to pray for material things. We have an all-knowing and all-powerful God. So why are we sure we know what to ask for? Instead, I should be praying more that God's will be done. God has a plan for me, and I'm sure it includes all that I need. God may give me what I was asking for, but boy, I don't know what else comes with that. I learned to end my prayers each day with phrases like, "Your will be done, not mine." I end every prayer with that as my reminder that He is God almighty. I want to glorify Him in my life. And boy, it's amazing how quickly peace comes upon me, and the rest of the things that at one point felt really hard and really challenging, don't seem so complicated anymore.

It isn't as hard as we make it out to be. It comes down to this: Are we willing to be so humble to acknowledge and give all the power to God? Do we believe in God almighty and that we were made with a purpose in mind? Do you believe that you're a son or daughter in Christ? Are you willing to believe He's in control, and through our faith we can experience all He has planned? If you let Him present the opportunities to you, the people He has placed in your life to influence you and if you look at why they're there, you may have a very different view of what you can do, who you can be, and what your purpose is. God orchestrated for you to encounter certain people in life. They're not there accidentally; He started planning a long time ago. I didn't meet Tony Jeary and Jim Norman on a plane in LaGuardia back in 2007 accidentally.

I know they were meant to be there.

Gratitude

I thank God every day for about six things: my physical health, my mental health, my financial resources, my family and friends, the opportunities He's presented to me, and for His Son, Jesus Christ, through whom we are saved, are forgiven and receive his grace. I try to keep it simple, because God already knows what we really need. I thank Him daily, because I realized that I don't always know when that moment He is orchestrating is going to arrive, but I know He's putting me in places to do things or to see things or experience things. If I open myself up to learn from those, I can see something potentially very powerful.

I would love to make a difference. Even if it's just for one person. That's a good enough why for Mark Mitchell. But I really believe God has given me more responsibility than that—to be a disciple of Jesus Christ and to serve others with humility and integrity and make a difference in their lives. Sometimes we won't know what impact we made that day, but I try to make a difference every day, and often the people I get to impact will say, "That was great. Thank you." I have aligned my heart with God's, and in seeking to make a difference every day, and seeing the impact that makes, gives me immense gratitude for all God has given me. I'm humbled at every opportunity to make a difference and help form leadership decisions and direction that will impact lots of people—customers and employees and every person I meet.

Not everyone thinks this way. Let's face it, there are a lot of people who don't feel this way about following Jesus and following that command to love. People pick and choose what they want to take away from Scripture and apply it to the side they have chosen. Then they want you to pick a side: Are you Democrat or Republican? Where do you stand on this or that issue? Everyone is going to encounter that person who wants to pound them down for the way that they follow Jesus.

If you find yourself in one of those conversations where someone begins to get really passionate, one of the most important things you can do is to participate in active listening. I try to understand why that person believes that way. We are all a collection of our experiences. I first try to understand their point of view, and secondly I acknowledge why their point is valid through their lens. One of the most relevant human feelings or needs is acknowledgement, and one of the worst is dismissal or to be minimalized. At a minimum, acknowledge that they exist, and their views are real. If we first seek to understand using active listening, then are willing to take a leap and acknowledge their point of view as valid through their lens—if we do those two things—we have a chance to teach, to educate, to share a new perspective, or to create a new experience. Change can occur or at least it can start.

Show an interest in them, then acknowledge that they feel that way for a reason. Then you've created that safe zone. You've created a safety net around this conversation, and boy, what can you do then? That's why relationships matter. In business you don't have to be friends, but you must have a friendly and trusted relationship to get things done and to make decisions in a timely, collaborative fashion.

What's that adage? "You'll catch more bees with honey than with vinegar." It's true. People who feel valued and cared for where they are will work harder and to make better decisions.

Inclusion and diversity are about a new set of thinking and experiences to share and about having people feel safe in an environment where they're valued and acknowledged. That's what inclusion and diversity are trying to accomplish in the world for people and for businesses.

Whatever those truths are that you want to hold to in life—your faith, your work perspective, your family views, whatever that is—these matter. Your point of view is comprised of the experiences that got you there. If you want to get to a better place, why wouldn't you open your mind to bring in the point of view of others who will help you get to that better place? It goes back to learning, right? We're learning from others and from life experiences, and continuous learning is how we all get to that best place to be the best us.

My Only Competition

I'm no longer competing with anybody else. It's just me. It changes everything.

To learn and get better and make more of a difference at work at home, I look at the roles that I play in life. I'm first a Christian. I'm a son, I'm a father, I'm a brother, I'm a husband, I'm an uncle, I'm a nephew, I'm a friend, I'm a leader. And I want to be the best Mark in all of these many roles. I want to be a great friend. I want to be an amazing father. I want to be a devoted husband. I want to be a passionate disciple of Jesus Christ.

There's a lot of aspiration there. But how else do I get there if I don't practice active listening and learning from the opportunities, while seeking the input of others and trying to get to a better place.

It takes a great deal of humility to be able to listen to the person you don't like or the combatants in the conference room. It takes a lot to open yourself up and be willing to learn from them.

While you may not learn a ton of positive things from the people you see as your enemies, for me, I know I have learned lessons about how not to be—even in those small moments of integrity or passion from people I did not care for. Your views, your beliefs morph, and change as you go. If you humble yourself and open yourself up to understand more about this world, it's a great step to get to a better place.

It's never too late to start learning nor start your path to faith and redemption.

Key Takeaways and Insights #4

Redemption Is Attainable

- How does this apply to you?

- What learning can you take away?

- Are you practicing the four tenants of biblical discipline, including: Scripture, traditions, reasoning, and being a part of a community of faith?
- Do you practice active listening every day?
- Do you know your purpose? Who you want to become?
- Do you invite inclusiveness and diversity into your life?

People,
Relationships,
and
Parenting

It's Not about Me (or You)!

This Insight offers a view on teams, an approach to serving others and our relationships.

During my time in college at Purdue University, I heard repeatedly that employees are the greatest asset for any business. When I started my career in business as an employee, I didn't hear that too often other than once or twice in a leadership speech. However, I can tell you that it is one of the most profound truths in business.

During this writing, I was leading what's called our HR shared services practice at American Airlines. That basically means that my team is accountable for driving the digital transformation—and a big part of the business transformation of the team—at American. It was very foundationally relevant because American's leadership since the merger of American and US Airways several years ago was and is keenly focused on the top corporate objectives, including building the right people-centered culture. Many of the things I was focused on with my team helped to drive and set the foundation for what that looks like for the future of American Airlines. We owned the systems (the digital transformation) which is how employees do business through SAP SuccessFactors, mobile application, and how they interact with us through our Team Member Service Center.

We were focused on the components of the employee experience and its support. We also had a team of vendor management and project management professionals who partnered with everyone else on the team. These team members helped drive transformation and build that culture the American Airlines is trying to cultivate. We were foundationally relevant in driving much of the people centered culture strategy at American for the years ahead.

Prior to that, in my previous three roles, I was able to drive strategy and leadership around different parts of the company. At one point I reported to the CMO (chief marketing officer) to help drive and formulate the new customer experience products and services at American Airlines. I've learned every step of the way, and through each new role and experience, I have grown and had the privilege of a very diverse and impactful career.

Earlier in my career, I spent roughly 17 years leading and running large airports and airport operations in various cities. Every position you take shapes you and prepares you for the next.

My last role before HR was the technology integration management role where I reported to the CIO. By association, I also had dotted line responsibility to the executive vice president of integration.

I was leading the technology integration management office for the first two years of the merger that ensured that

American had the right priorities, the right dependencies, and the correct strategy to integrate the technologies and bring two companies together for revenue, for customers, and for operations.

Ultimately when that was on track and successful, I was asked to help lead the employee strategy, technology, and business transformation of the company.

In the earliest part of my career, I was an industrial engineer who worked in airline planning. I also worked in the budgets and costs center of finance. But whenever people asked what my ultimate goal was, I would say that I was interested in learning about airport operations. The only problem was that my career path was headed in a different direction. I wanted to go do operations, and I finally got a chance to when I convinced our vice president at DFW (Dallas-Fort Worth) to throw me out to the wolves. In a few months I was in passenger services at DFW—one of the largest airports in the world. I started working the night shift at DFW with approximately 300 people under my jurisdiction, leading an afternoon shift at DFW, and managing ice, snow, rain thunderstorms, departure issues—you name it. Soon I would be working in the operations tower, then running the operations tower, which was literally getting paid to sit ten floors up in the sky and watch airplanes take off all day. That's an oversimplification, but it was a great job.

Every position taught me a new skill from the people I was blessed to work with and learn from.

It was really cool to literally be working in the nerve center of American Airlines' largest operation at the time: 500 plus flights a day, and my team was leading that from a hub operations perspective. Next, I got to go lead the ramp service organization, which at the time was an organization of 3,000 employees at DFW. We were responsible for everything that you see outside the window of a plane: handling baggage and loading the plane, mail and cargo, and cleaning aircraft, and all those critical operational functions.

There was a point in my Dallas tenure, about ten years in, when I was dying to run my own airport. I was gifted the opportunity to go run LaGuardia Airport in 1999. I was privileged to run that for the next three years during which time there was the very significant event of 9/11.

How does any leader navigate chaos that occurs externally? Every organization has some sort of external event at some point or another that will test the skills you have spent your career building.

Has this ever happened to you?

When 9/11 happened, nothing like it had ever happened before in the airline business, let alone our country. That Tuesday in New York was a long one, as were the days and weeks that followed. So much uncertainty was present, and at times it was chaotic. Yet, if offered me an incredible journey as the leader of New York's LaGuardia Airport for American Airlines that has impacted me for the many years that follow. It revealed who I was as a leader and showed the character of the individual that I had become.

Next, I was to lead an entire region of 26 cities alongside our regional partner, American Eagle, up in the northeast. Shortly after that, I went from a nice, complicated large airport, LaGuardia, to an even larger airport, LAX, our fourth largest airport at American, and I got to hang out in LA for a couple years before I was brought back into headquarters.

I was blessed to get to do lots of cool things in my career at

American Airlines, and I've been able to see very clearly that my gift in business is about knowing how to connect to and build relationships with people.

What Business Are We In?

Years ago, when our executive vice president was having a conversation with many on her staff, she asked, "What business are we in?" I was the only one in the room who didn't say something about airplanes. I offered to her that we are in the "people business," and through those people, we would deliver a great customer service. We'd fly airplanes and do all kinds of cool things.

My first gift is the understanding of the value of people and those relationships, and secondly, we get things done, we deliver results to drive the company to a better place. I would add that a third gift is my experience. I've gotten to touch lots of parts of the company. I know that individually, I may not be an expert in any one area, but the aggregate is the gift of lots and lots of relationships, lots and lots of experiences, lots and lots of opportunities to bring perspective, which helps me be more effective each role that I'm in.

In every organization I've touched over the years with the teams that I've led, we have delivered results. I know that results matter.

You don't need to have all the answers. But you can learn and get mentored along the way, just as I've been blessed by many great teachers and learned lots of lessons in my life about people and about results. But at the end of the day, it all comes back to people and how those people were willing to teach me, and now I can capture some of this wisdom and things I have learned to pay it forward. Your wisdom is a gift! Mentor others!

When you gift back to people and they can apply knowledge to themselves to be better people, it makes the world around them better too. It's returning that gift I learned from my father many, many years ago about giving back.

We are constantly learning whether we admit it or not. It's hard not to think about, *What if I knew that back then? What if I knew that at a younger age? What if I knew about applying work principles to my personal life? What if I knew about the value of faith and the hope that having a relationship with Jesus Christ brings? What if I knew the power of daily prayer? What happens with the power of relationships when I was twenty, and it wasn't all about me? What if I knew that then?* There's something to this as I think about wisdom and a lifetime of learning all wrapped up into this one simple book that you can read. It's about sharing with others the wealth of experience and wisdom that I've gained along the journey.

Key Takeaways and Insights #5

It's Not about Me (or You)!

- How does this apply to you?

- What can you take away?

- People matter. It's about all the others in our lives! Are you serving others?
- Learning comes from experiences and especially from acts of service.
- Teams matter.
- What gift can you pass on to others?
- What can you do to improve and broaden the key relationships in your life?

INSIGHT #6

Be the Best You

This Insight challenges you to stop competing against others. You are not in competition with anyone other than who you used to be; focus on becoming a better you!

Every individual, parent, and leader is responsible for their own personal development. Some seek out coaches and mentors, and others read, attend seminars, or take on challenging new projects. What do you do, in order to be the very best person and leader that you can be?

If you haven't asked yourself that question, now is as good a time as any.

Throughout life, every one of us is challenged at different parts of our journey with identity and growth. Every stage of life is different. In college and into our twenties, we may not yet know who we are or who we want to be. That's OK! But at every stage, we can strive to be our best.

In my roles within American Airlines, I've often been in a position to help encourage others to grow and develop their careers. There's no greater honor than leading someone to a new level and seeing the reward of their growth. But ultimately, whether they act on your feedback is up to them. Don't hold yourself responsible for someone else's decision to grow.

Personal leadership is an inside job.

Every day comes with a moment where we will be challenged and sometimes tested to be the best human possible. When times are challenging and difficult, it's extremely easy to take a detour away from giving your best and being your best. Every day is packed with to-do lists, meetings, and conference calls. These are your planned events let alone what happens when unplanned calls or issues arise during the day and totally overtake even the best planned days. Regardless, it is important that you start each day with a commitment and self-confidence that being the "best you" will be all that is needed. It sometimes takes trial by fire to discover being something other than that is a disaster in the making. The question is, Do you really know what is the "best you"?

Values

What are your core values? Everyone travels through different stages of growth, but if you haven't taken time to think about the values that are important to you, action will be based on external factors. People without defined core values often react and respond to others.

Without values as your foundation (your anchors), the way you conduct your day, and your ability to be effective at the highest level, will just be unintentional actions or good ideas.

One of my values is intentionality. I want to have extreme clarity about everything I do. One of my mentors, Tony Jeary, coaches leaders to achieve Clarity, Focus, and Execution. He's coached some of the top leaders and CEOs in the world to be the best they can be. This intentionality has helped me personally at work and at home in key areas of my life.

One of the things I do each day is to establish my goals.

I have daily goals, weekly goals, monthly goals, and annual goals. I establish these on an ongoing basis for both my personal life and professional life. It helps me create a foundation for keeping me focused on the things that matter and centered on things that are aligned with my values and principles. What I also have discovered is that achieving goals brings me joy and some degree of happiness. When you set goals, you feel more in control of your life, and it provides a sense of freedom because you've got a plan.

The sense of accomplishment when I achieve a goal feeds my confidence, but the planning process itself helps too.

What I have found over the years is that the goals that I establish and how I go about achieving them say a lot about my character. If you looked over my written goals, you could probably easily identify my purpose and write it down in very few words. Knowing my purpose enables me to connect all those activities and goals to who I want to be and be known for. Together they make up the "best me" possible. At the end of the month, I look back to see how I did. This process helps me to chart a path using the "best me" as the beacon and lighthouse.

What Does Your Perfect Month Look Like?

Whenever I am asked to discuss career goals with a fellow employee or mentor, I always begin with self-reflection: Do you believe **today** that you are the *best you*? Most of the people I ask this question usually squirm a bit in their seat because the real question imbedded in there is, "Do you know who you are?" Most people want to better understand how to improve their career trajectory, or life in general, yet ultimately the journey almost always leads back to the question, What kind of person do you want to be? Since the dawn of time, humans have contemplated the meaning of their lives.

If this sounds like you, it's perfectly normal.

Do you ever wonder why you're here?

Why you exist?

What your purpose is?

Would you regret things if you never understand your purpose?

The answers may shock you. I have found that most people don't really know who they are or what their purpose is. Turning the question around, they know who they don't want to be but usually have little idea of who they are. This type of personal self-reflection takes some time and energy. In my years in leadership I have discovered that many people never really do this or take the time to self-reflect. It must be done to be able to chart a course for knowing how to achieve the "best you"! How else would you know if you are being true to the person you most want to be?

Goals are great, but a goal without a purpose is meaningless. It's important to live with purpose.

Most people describe their best self as achieving success or pursuing some type of interest—as if the "best you" is only connected to achievement. Digging a little deeper, they then connect their "best you" with achievement and the experience of joy. I challenge them to think differently when I can. Is the best you a pursuit of happiness? Joy? Success?

I would offer that your goal in life shouldn't be about the pursuit of happiness but the pursuit of living a life of purpose.

Your purpose in life should be about living the kind and type of life that God intended you to live. So, what is your purpose? Do you believe that your life really matters? It's a big question, but one our God wants you to actively seek out.

There are some things about your purpose that apply to everyone, and I learned them from my parents. God's purpose for you shouldn't be a competition against other people, though achieving your meaning in life will include other people. Setting goals to be a better you only makes the most sense when you start with knowing what your purpose is.

God gives you your purpose, and it is counterproductive to give only a little of control to God to reshape your life. Give it all to Him!

To be psychologically and spiritually healthy, we need to believe that our lives matter. Why else would you exist unless it was to accomplish something important while you are here? For you to live out your God-given purpose, you need to discover ways to feel connected to something larger than yourself. Simply put, your purpose is not about a promotion or level of responsibility. These are good, but they are only activities at work or items you collect and buy. Significance matters. Each one of us wants to feel significant and be driven by purpose.

For your life to have meaning you must believe you are part of something bigger than just yourself.

The Obstacles of Purpose

With nearly 35 years in leadership, I have discovered there are several things that always seem to get in the way and keep people from enjoying their purpose.

1. Failure

Some never find their purpose or walk in it because they have a fear of failure. Does failing make you worry about what other people think about you? Failure is part of life. Failure can provide invaluable lessons so long as progress is made in your discovering your purpose and discovering the best you possible. Failure can provide important steps in development that prepare you for future success. Most of the time, what you experience is not really failure but more like setback or lesson that can be taken forward to new experiences. The real question is, Did the failure you experienced deviate you from your values? How you persevere and learn for these moments really develops character and lets you discover how important your values are. Without those critical learning moments, you would miss out on the potential to learn and not benefit from the experience. You would never progress into all that you can be.

Are your failures learning moments for you?

Perhaps one of the worst things you can do about these learning experiences is not to own them. I have met many managers and supervisors that will never accept their role in these learning moments. They are always the result of someone else's errors. Blame is the kiss of death! You must face reality and own your involvement. Without this there is no learning moment. You must take personal responsibility, even if it's a small portion to be better the next time. These moments of failure or learning moments are times when you take ground or give ground—personally and professionally. It all depends on how you respond to them.

2. Fear of Success

Some people associate success with something bad. Anything

based on fear is not about your purpose in life. Fear is a spirit, and it's not from your Creator. Anxiety is sometimes disguised as fear or misinterpreted as fear. Anxiety can be a good thing, especially if it exists as a signal that you may be in danger or approaching a bad situation.

Fear that keeps you from your purpose is not from God and is always a lie. It's important that these moments of fear be overcome. If not, they will always pop up at the worst moments and possibly keep you from discovering joy, happiness, and your purpose in life. If there is one thing I know, it is that your future is coming. Will you be ready to embrace all that God has for you?

More importantly, are you prepared to be positive, open-minded, and good to yourself? Negative self-talk almost always comes from your past experiences. Many times, it has nothing to do with reality. If you are reminding yourself that you are a failure, I can tell you that is not true.

Understanding the reason why these thoughts reappear is critical since they can then be pruned from your "best you"! All I can say is that most critical talk is never true, and it needs to stay in your past. Letting negative self-talk impede living out your purpose only anchors you to lies. All lies of the enemy must be overcome. Negative talk about others, or even about yourself, never does anyone any good. Playing the victim card is never attractive and is never a path to success. Being known as a negative person will be a showstopper in terms of your career. Today companies look for people who are motivators and can work in diverse teams.

3. Procrastination
Stop procrastination, which leads to feeling or thinking

that you're not prepared.

Training and preparation are important, but I have learned that you will never be fully prepared for all the circumstances that you will face. What is critical is that you understand that learning is a lifelong process, and sometimes God will place you in a circumstance that you may not be perfectly qualified for. What God does know is that your faith and hard work will pull you through, and others around you will also benefit from your attitude and commitment. Sometimes moments can be too big for you. This is when you can rely on your team, mentors, and other like-minded friends and colleagues. Understanding who you are, what your values are, and how they can be reflected in the culture is most important. When this occurs, you and your team will respond to almost any challenge and rise above to excel and exceed expectations.

Starting today, promise to be the **best version of you**!

By every conceivable measure, life here in America is getting better and better, yet at the same time, depression, suicide, and hopelessness continue to rise. What's missing from our lives that has caused this increase in loneliness and negativity? It is the human connection and seeking to be more in your purpose every day. Where you are in your journey doesn't matter because you can choose to make meaningful relationships, and the pursuit of your purpose a priority. Your age and place in life don't matter either!

My parents are in their eighties and continue to lead very active lives. When I visit them, their home telephone—yes, the one with a cord attached to the wall—continues to ring. Almost always it involves an issue with another family or someone connected to the church that needs support. Whenever they answer the telephone, they are 100 percent present in the conversation and very instrumental in solving problems and helping those on the other end.

I believe they are living out their purpose in life, and they both love it and are happier than ever! They have many long-term relationships with other people and couples they can count on. I constantly hear from other people what a blessing they are to the people around them. This never impacts them one way or another. They just keep a servant mentality and do all that is possible to help others. There is definitely a connection to living a purpose-filled life and happiness. How do you give back?

Growing up I vividly remember the sense of anticipation my parents had every day getting ready to head off to work while my siblings and I prepared for school. I don't remember moments of stress or fits of depression when my parents lost their cool or went on a rant.

Over the years I thought a lot about my parents and the lessons they gave to me, most of which was demonstrated in their daily lives. I recently came across a study called the Harvard Study of Adult Development, which is also accompanied by a "TED Talk" released in 2015. The TED talk was called "Good relationships keep us happier and healthier" and was released by the study's current director Dr. Robert Waldinger. The Harvard Study is considered one of the world's longest studies of adult life and was started in 1938 during the Great Depression. Dr. Waldinger is a psychiatrist and the fourth director of the ongoing Harvard study.

"The Harvard study has shown that the people who fared the best, in terms of health and happiness, were the people who leaned into relationships, with family, with friends, with community," Waldinger said. The study has been ongoing and spans over 81 years of participants. Researchers tracked the lives of 724 men, following up with each one on an annual basis to ask about their work, home lives, and health.

The research was quite detailed and included years of onsite interviews involving other family members in their homes like spouses and children. The study included reviews of their physical well-being and medical records, blood analysis, and in-depth and regular check points.

In his TED Talk Waldinger said, "The clearest message from the study is that good relationships keep us happier and healthier." The social aspects to life and the quality of relationships are what keep us happy and healthy in our later stages in life.

Simply stated, people with friends live longer and are happier than those who are more isolated and not fully involved in life. Becoming social is important to longevity.

In Dr. Waldinger's TED Talk, he highlighted another study of millennials who were asked what some of their most important life goals were. It was a little surprising when over 80 percent of them said that a major goal for them was to get rich. They connected the goal of becoming rich to happiness. It was all about money. In the same study, Dr. Waldinger claimed that over 50 percent of the same young people said another goal was to become famous. Rich and famous equaled happiness.

How can you argue with this notion or find fault in this thinking when even primary schools and corporate environments connect today's quest for happiness to a focus on work and achievement? This distorted bombardment is constant and endless! Ads and marketing messages connecting happiness and purpose to obtaining more stuff is everywhere you look. Somewhere along the way, having a good life has been infiltrated by working longer hours and receiving promotions and collecting material things. This is not good path and almost juxtaposed to living a purpose-filled life and experiencing happiness.

I've had a terrific corporate career that has some achievements that I am very proud of, but I don't think my career or my achievements are what defines me. My bank account is fuller than my parents could imagine, but although the things it allows me to do may bring me moments of happiness, it hardly provides me the meaning for my life or why I think I am here. Don't get me wrong! I love what I do, but it's not how I want to be remembered. I would not want my career to be my legacy after my earthly life is over. Rather, how I interact at my job and how I treated people should say something about who I am and what I am about. How I relate to my subordinates, peers, and executive team provides some insight about me as a human being and what I stand for. I want my legacy to be about the impact I've had on the people around me. Not just at the office but at the local 7-11, the credit union, and the dry cleaners. Every day, I choose to create the legacy I want, and you can too. The work and achievements I accomplish here are not why I am here—but they do say something about who I am.

The legacy I am leaving behind is a purposeful achievement. I have identified my values that I want to be known for and work to always portray them in all my dealings and relationships. This gives people comfort in knowing what I am all about. Remember those daily, weekly, and monthly goals that I establish? They keep me focused and on track to establishing that legacy. Within the goals are business goals, personal goals, workout goals, and financial goals. But you can also find goals about getting better at connecting with people and helping my team achieve more and have more fun. Living a meaningful life is an ongoing process. My parents are still working on it and are the best example for me.

It's the everyday of life that matters. How do you want to be remembered?

For most people, your memory, your legacy will be comprised of only a few moments. These moments will define the memory of your life. These usually are major moments that encapsulate your character and purpose together. Looking around, you can always find good examples and even bad examples. Both are good to observe.

As I've said earlier, it's important to mentor and be mentored. Mentors are also important and are good to pursue. I've had some great ones along the way. Some I met with monthly, and some mentors I just observed from a distance. Either way they were good examples of how to interact—or not interact—and helped me tremendously along the way. On the contrary, people who are isolated more often live shorter lives. The importance of the depth and quality of your close relationships is at an all-time high.

The good news is, there is still time.

There is an endless list of organizations that can use help. This can be by donating your time as a volunteer or sometimes as a paid helper. The bottom line is, there are plenty of opportunities to connect with some other organization and get involved with things that are larger than yourself. Get involved and make a difference! See how it changes you.

Mother Teresa said, "The good you do today will be forgotten. Do good anyway. Give the world the best you have, and it may never be enough. Give the world the best you've got anyway."

One last quote: "All great achievements have sprung from the fountain of enthusiasm, by people consumed with earnestness of purpose, with confidence in themselves, with faith in the worthwhileness of their endeavors" (B. C. Forbes).

Key Takeaways and Insights #6

Be the Best You

- How does this apply to you?

- What learning can you take away?

- Do you have a mentor or coach? Are these meaningful relationships? What would they say about you?
- Are you intentional with your daily activities?
- Do you know your values? Have you written them down for clarity?
- Do you know your purpose?
- Do you volunteer your time at a local charity?

Demonstrate Love

*This Insight offers that in life and
in leadership, love matters!*

Love is the highest of all values we can possess in life and in business. The investment of love in others is not only the most valuable gift you can give, but it changes generations when you pour love, kindness, and mentorship into others.

Do You Care about Your Teams?

Mentoring is part of leadership, I have talked at length about securing a mentor for your own life, but now it is time to give back to others what you have had the opportunity to learn. If you don't think you have anything to share, I assure you that is a lie from the enemy. Your love and time poured into someone else could impact their entire life. Your story isn't like anyone else's. Mentorship is important to me, and I have been mentoring a young team member who was on the edge of turning thirty. It started as a once-a-month meeting, talking about the different career paths that would be available to him, and what paths he could take for his future. I invest time in him because I care about his future.

But recently the meetings and dialogue started to turn into more like life mentoring. He is in a relationship with a lovely young lady, and our talks have begun to expand into many different areas. We've talked about the financial market, the housing market, views on bank loans, and different types of investing. We even discussed his goals to have their first child and start a family. Even a friendship or same-sex mentorship or colleague relationship can be delivered in love.

True love means that you understand that it is unconditional and about investing in others. It means that I will love you no matter what. True love is sacrificial. I will give up things I want for you. I will make sacrifices for you. Most importantly, and probably the hardest part of true love is forgiveness. True love is forgiving, and it is critical to have that perspective. You must be able to say, "I forgive you." No, it isn't easy. It's hard. I've experienced that in my life. A lot of my learning about love, the phases of love, and what true love is comes from pain and failures with those I loved. My divorce for a long time felt like a failure of major proportions.

After my divorce, I reframed my thinking a lot as I focused on thinking of ways I could become a better human. As a parent, the foundation of true love is easy. You brought the child into the world, and you are going to love that child unconditionally. You are going to make sacrifices by nature by being a parent, and your kids are going to make mistakes. Through youthful mistakes, you're going to forgive them. It's sometimes harder in our marital relationship because, as an adult, you have to put someone else first and truly understand why you're making a sacrifice for someone else. Does the other person understand your sacrifice? Do you understand theirs? Understanding that sacrifice is relevant for both parties.

In my first marriage, there was a period of making some choices that were not very good. I wanted the relationship to work, but it didn't.

Even in some of the lowest most painful moments in our married life, I found myself willing to help, to understand, to acknowledge the challenge and work through it. And in every case, I was always willing to figure out a path forward. I was also very forgiving. A deeper understanding of forgiveness came during that period. I understood more why God wants to forgive us.

My experiences during that time helped me frame the perspective of the three phases of love. Most relationships start out immersed in the fun, loving, cuddly, "you're cute" stage. It's a time when you don't stop thinking about each other. You have an attraction toward each other, and you have fun together so you want to be together.

It always starts with some kind of romance and excitement. Add in some happy hormones, and you become bonded. The more of that fun and emotional bonding that you do, the more that it becomes something you want daily. That bonding ultimately leads to a commitment. You each commit to see just one another. Then commit to each other as a couple. You move through the natural course that every relationship goes through from dating to engagement, and eventually, you both make a commitment at the altar and get married.

Maybe it happens slowly or maybe a crisis comes along and throws a wrench in your bliss. You get to a point where it's not easy anymore. It has actually gotten hard. The fun isn't there like it has been, and it begins to feel like work. Life gets hard, kids come along—whatever the challenge is doesn't matter. What matters is how you as a person and how you both as a couple choose to respond to those challenges. We may make all kinds of choices that can lead to a good or bad outcomes, and even moments that require apologies and forgiveness. What people need to know (and it may seem simple enough) is that relationships aren't easy.

Sadly, in America today, the facts would say that some 50 percent of marriages end in divorce. It is a sad and unfortunate choice. It can seem easier to give up than to rekindle and recommit. Divorce happens, but it's a choice that is made. Divorce isn't something that just happens in marriage. Through the years, I have seen relationships broken up when conflict arises and someone decides it's easier to walk away. Sometimes walking away in certain scenarios is not necessarily wrong, but let's acknowledge that it's something that you choose and really drives the outcomes and consequences that we get.

Everyone is allowed to make their own choices. It's important to understand that with choice comes consequence, and consequence will alter the results that you ultimately achieve.

When it gets hard, you need to be willing to make a choice to recommit. To redefine the cuddly and emotionally cool and fun part of your relationship. To remember what helped you find each other and build that love in the first place. To take those memories and build on what you used to know about each other. You both made choices. It always comes with a choice. Love is a feeling first. Love is a commitment second. Love is a choice.

Key Takeaways and Insights #7

Demonstrate Love

• How does this apply to you?

• What learning can you take away?

• How can you demonstrate love today?

• Phases of relationships include the three Cs:
  > Cute and Cuddly
  > Commitment
  > Choice

• What choice do you make when your relationships face difficult moments and adversity? True love is:
  > Unconditional
  > Sacrificial
  > Forgiving—"Mercy trumps judgement."

• Are you practicing all three of these?

When it's hard I encourage you to remember this:
"Even though I walk through the darkest valley, I will fear no evil; for you are with me" (Psalm 23:4).

And this too:

"Those who hope in the LORD will renew their strength. They will soar on wings like eagles; they will run and not grow weary; they will walk and not be faint" (Isaiah 40:31).

Relationships Matter

This Insight offers that relationships matter and shares an approach to ensuring yours are in the best shape for you!

No one is perfect. I know this isn't a newsflash for you, but it is something that can help us see our relationships with more grace. We all are going to make mistakes. When these mistakes hurt other people, or someone hurts you, it is critical that you develop a willingness to forgive.

Sometimes that may be hard to do, but forgiveness is what sets you free to be your genuine self as God made you to be. Unforgiveness rarely hurts the person who hurt you. Harboring unforgiveness only inhibits you from experiencing the freedom and joy that God wants you to experience. That is one of the things you can learn about relationships that also applies in business.

Why did you build a relationship with your boss and your coworkers? We are all human, and by nature of being a human, we are imperfect, and we are going to make mistakes, and we're going to do things that sometimes don't even make sense to ourselves! I had to work through being able to forgive. I consciously tried to take myself to a better place regarding forgiveness, and I think it's an art that I have, but it had to be developed. It did not come naturally, but I have grown considerably and had more positive outcomes by being able to forgive. It's something I've learned to negotiate circumstances through and realize the importance of and directly benefit from. The key is keeping the perspective of valuing the relationship over the event.

When you consider what the person's intention was, you should be able more easily to pave a path forward. Sometimes people do intentionally hurtful things. But it's my choice as to how it impacts me, and it's my choice as to how the consequences affect me going forward.

Sometimes the best choice is to walk away. Step back and think more about the why behind what happened versus how angry you are. You will find this perspective refreshing and leads toward cooperation and compromise that will enable you to rebuild the relationship and create a path forward. Understanding the "why" and drilling down into that really brings to light an interesting perspective and understanding. With that understanding comes the realization that you have a choice how you respond. One of your most complete choices and the healthiest to choose is that you can forgive, and then move forward.

Let's be clear, forgiveness works for both people, but forgiveness doesn't mean that what someone did was OK. Forgiveness is a gift you give yourself. It's not just a way to build trust and respect in a relationship. It's also for the toxic people you must let go. Some things don't have any business being part of your life at all. You must be able to forgive those people and let them go and be OK with the fact that maybe nothing ever happened that redeemed them of what happened to you. Forgiveness is not letting them off the hook. You're letting yourself off the hook and giving yourself a chance to grow and heal and move forward.

Christ gave us a pretty good example of the power of forgiveness. You always should aspire to be something better. You are not going to achieve that without being better at the act of forgiving. As part of my Christian faith, we had a pretty good teacher, and the act of forgiveness should be easier for us to exercise, the ability to forgive people when they are wrong should be what we seek because that is what Christ did for us.

Resolving Conflict

When Gina and I started to go through the engagement process, there was a key difference that came up. One of them was she was raised in the Catholic Church, and I was raised in the United Methodist Church. When we began planning our wedding, I asked her where she wanted to get married. We made the decision to go to New Orleans. She wanted to get married in the Catholic Church, and because I had been previously married, we began the process of what the Catholic Church required for us to get married—an annulment of my first marriage.

The entire concept was foreign to me, and the annulment process with the Catholic Church seemed awkward. It took several meetings into it before I began to truly understand what they were asking me to do. Once I understood what was happening, I needed to have an honest conversation with Gina. It began like this: "I'm really struggling with this annulment process. I'm not in agreement with what the Catholic

Church is asking me to do. They are asking me to acknowledge my previous marriage was a mistake I made."

"My first marriage wasn't a mistake," I said. "I was married for eighteen years and produced two amazing children. Obviously, the marriage ended, but dragging me through the past and asking me to acknowledge things that I don't think are accurate is not productive." I continued, "It's not good to bring my ex-wife and to bring my kids into that conversation with the Catholic Church and struggle to see how it is going to help us as husband and wife."

Within a minute, Gina quietly answered, "I understand that, and I'm good with the past and agree with how you're feeling."

She could have held firm that she needed this for her to marry me. But she listened to me, heard me, and compromised. Her ability to not be held to a church principle, but to compromise, and to be open to collaboration, and try to understand how we can move forward beyond this rules-based setback was endearing. And I was then and still am eternally grateful for her and for that moment. Her seeing my side was a moment of true love.

"Then where should we get married?" I asked. "How should we do this?"

She immediately responded, "Let's have your dad marry us!"

My dad was a retired principal and now is an ordained pastor.

I smiled and said, "Wow, that's powerful. Yeah, let's do it!" That just shows that if you are true to the commitment and true to the relationship, you can work through difficult things, even something as important as a religious difference. My dad was honored to marry us, and it was kind of fun going through the counseling with him. How many people have your dad counsel you as a soon-to-be married couple?

Together, Gina and I worked through what could have been potentially a very powerful disconnect. The commitment was there. We made a choice to move forward together and build on the strengths of the spiritual commonalities between Catholicism and the United Methodist Church. Both being Christian, we built on the strengths rather than worrying about the differences.

The importance of forgiveness and the decision to forgive someone else isn't just for someone else. It's for you. The real benefit of forgiveness is for the person giving forgiveness. It's for your benefit. Holding a grudge against someone really doesn't impact their life. It only impacts the one who is grudging! I am sure you have heard the cliché, "Holding a grudge is like drinking poison and expecting the other person to die." Forgiving someone allows you to not hold on to the pain or resentment. It's allows you to move and focus on the future. If you hold on to things of the past, and you don't forgive, you will stay stuck right there. It also allows us to realize there's something more important—in this case an opportunity to hear Gina say, "I'm good."

I've watched people who can't be on the forgiving side, and it really becomes a major distractor, not just with the person they're trying to forgive. Then it becomes a bigger thorn in their next relationship and the next relationship.

Carrying emotional resentment into your new relationships will just cause repeat problems and collateral issues. Letting go of the burden is incredibly powerful and incredibly important to the healing process.

Forgiveness is important in the corporate world too. Especially when you believe the company has done something negative to you. Maybe you didn't get that raise, or your performance review was bad. Perhaps you were skipped over for a promotion.

What about in the event of a mistake that could nearly cost you the position at your job?

When someone makes a mistake and finds him- or herself on a probationary period in order for the company to see that they have corrected their behavior, there can be anger and resentment, even when that person understands the "why" behind the probation. For the employee on probation, it's critical not to hold on to resentment, but to understand that the organization is still wanting to contribute into their lives, whether it's training or mentoring, or to create a plan for improvement.

It's best to look at all feedback (and even reprimands) as an opportunity. The choice is yours as is how you use it. It can be seen as an opportunity for improvement, or you can choose to find no value in the feedback, and it will probably just hurt your career. When you're able to put yourself into a healthy perspective and get past the emotion of, "My boss wronged me, or this person said something hurtful," good things can happen.

You can make the choice to learn from that and the choice to also find that path forward again. This is very true in the workforce. When you accept the negative feedback, or the performance review that isn't so good, or the probationary program that you're on, you absolutely can then pave a path forward.

I can think of two or three employees in my career who

were on a probationary plan with strict criteria for continued employment. I'll never forget when I was in New York and was running LaGuardia airport and had an employee who I knew did something very wrong (it was worthy of termination). The union basically said, "Please give him a second chance." So we gave the employee a second chance.

I knew I wanted to give this some careful thought. If the guy made a mistake again, then it would be very easy to then take the company action that was required and let him go. Nobody would fault me or the company then, and it would prove that management does listen and is flexible. It would signal that management and the union were aligned for the common good.

By giving him that chance, he had the opportunity to become a model citizen and turn it around. Guess what? He did turn it around, and he was a model citizen for the entire time I stayed in New York. Sometimes when you give people a second chance, they realize that redemption is an opportunity and forgiveness is an opportunity, great things can happen.

During a performance review, as we were contemplating helping a problematic employee to exit the company, we decided to wait. What if he has good intentions? Maybe we can coach around the performance issues. So we created a documented performance improvement plan for him.

A year later, while the guy's not a superstar yet, he's made incredible improvements. He's earned a pay increase this year which is a positive thing for anyone working in a company. Both of those employees were willing to take the feedback as an opportunity, and the company was willing to forgive and overlook some of the past and move forward and pave that path forward together.

We created an environment for these two people and gave them a chance to move forward. People can recover from setbacks.

Adversity and Integrity

Adversity reveals character. Integrity is who you are when nobody's watching. But when you're in the middle of adversity, be that at work or home, it reveals the character and the values that you stand for. Your reaction when adversity arrives, or a setback happens, is a test of your character. It isn't *if* setbacks happen, it's *when* because they will happen. Your character was framed over many years through different experiences. If you think about and believe the person you marry, or the person you employed is of good character, it really changes how you think about giving that second chance as well and being willing to forgive. It's also a reflection of your own character.

Most of the people reading this book will have lived half of a lifetime already. If you're one who is having trouble figuring things out, forgiving, and moving forward, you're wasting time. Time is a resource you can't get back. Everyone's got some part of their history or their story they're painfully aware of, and it's kept them from enjoying life to the fullest. Some things must be let go.

Forgiveness is the gift of letting go. It's not living in something that's over. When we're trapped in unforgiveness, we're reliving something that has already happened. It's like running a race while carrying a large heavy box with you.

How can we forgive and let go? One of the first steps is to try to see and understand the other person's perspective. Once you understand the intent, that allows you to gain a whole new perspective on how big of a deal it is. One of the things that I always try to say: "Why did that person do that to me, or why do I think they did that to me?" If you seek to understand the source of the incident, you can understand if the intention was hurtful or it may be something less egregious.

Your life has the risk of being consumed with the negativity that you can't let go of. If you miss opportunities to move forward, not just from that particular relationship or events, but in general, you will risk being consumed. I've witnessed that in other people and in some of my personal relationships.

Many times the incident has not only created the need for forgiveness, but it has now created another problem. A lack of trust. Our thoughts can range from, "What if they hurt me again?" or, "What if this person doesn't love me the same?"

Holding onto this baggage runs the risk of inhibiting or impacting other relationship that you have in the future, especially when it comes to a second marriage, your second girlfriend, or a second boyfriend. When you bring your broken perception to a new relationship, you put that new person at risk when you are unable to be the best you. If your life has been filled with negativity, it will be difficult to flourish in that second chance you've been given. I was fortunate in my second marriage. It's proof that new relationships can flourish when you allow yourself to let go and put aside any of the negativity.

Our lives have limitless potential, and it is not only sad, but to some degree tragic, to watch people who can't get past hurts or events and stay trapped in the pain. It's really a forgiveness opportunity. I know that I make it sound as if this is easy, but as much as I am thoughtful about how I try to think about this, and how I really try to be introspective and see my role in it as well, I was challenged with a forgiveness opportunity.

It was a hard choice to make, even when I knew it was the best outcome for me.

Nearly ten years ago, during American's corporate restructuring, something happened to me that felt like an injustice. At some level I've healed, but it still was able to have an impact on me. I shared it with my new boss, a new vice president who came into the company about a year ago. I shared it with him recently, and he asked me this question, which was very thoughtful on his part: "How does someone who's been through those series of events that you just described still work here?"

Then he said, "How do you get past that, and why are you still here?"

That's a great question that even though he was just getting to know me, it was a natural response to for him to question why I stayed and why I work through those issues. I also appreciated him asking an open-ended question that allowed me to discuss it more deeply and potentially recommit to him. He asked me that question as we were just getting to know each other better. This type of issue presents a powerful question and not unsimilar when couples or spouses, male or female, experience an issue that requires one of you to have to get over it and be able make a way back to trust their spouse again.

The relationship with my new boss, Cornelius, is something that we have been consciously working on over the last year or so in a very positive way. We talk as much about our similar health interests, my personal travels, and our sports interests as much as we talk about the current business challenges we have. Each one on one starts with a deck of cards. We just randomly choose one of the cards in the deck of 52, and it has a question or a thought-provoking statement, like,

"What's your favorite restaurant you haven't tried?" or, "What was the most significant events in your life that shaped who you are?" They're random questions. As he and I have matured into our relationship, there is now a certain new level of trust that exists that now allows us to have different conversations versus what we talked about a year ago when he was my new boss. It takes time and it takes trust.

Every one of the cards that he has is a conversation starter that reveals a little bit about the person who's drawing the card out of the deck. It's interesting how it starts off all our meetings on a very personal note, but also allows the business conversation to be more effective. The depth and openness of the relationship has enabled better dialogue and a better process that leads to better decisions, personally and professionally.

At the last meeting we had, we started the meeting, and I said, "Is something wrong? I don't get to draw a card today." He chuckled and spread the cards on his desk, and I reached over and flipped one of the cards over. I smiled as I read the card silently to myself, *What do you do when things don't go your way and you know you're right?* It's how we start the meeting; we always open with something personal. I know it's coming from an inanimate source; and it works even better as an ice breaker because it feels even less personal, but it gives you an opportunity to be personal.

It took the team at American Airlines somewhere between nine and ten months to get Cornelius through the executive review before we were ready to hire him. I was one of the first to interview him. It was I and another colleague discussing some of his qualifications and running some situations by him in the interview. At the conclusion of the interview, my colleague and I sat back and discussed some feedback. We both looked at each other after the meeting, and said, "He's the one, he's our new boss!" I just knew right then he was the right fit culturally and professionally, and he checked all the boxes plus some.

I think back into my life about relationships, and my first memory of relationships was at four or five years old. I have fond memories of how I spent time with my cousins, especially at holidays like Thanksgiving and Christmas. Like most people, my cousins were my first best friends, and it really shaped how I started to think about other people in my life and why they mattered. As kids we would run around the historic battlegrounds near West Lafayette, Indiana. We'd run around while the parents visited and stayed inside. My dad is one of nine children, and he's the youngest. You can imagine how many cousins would show up at Thanksgiving holiday meal. We would have as many as a hundred people at Thanksgiving dinner.

Each Thanksgiving we rented out a campground facility, and our family would stay there. We would have 40 or 50 cousins of varying ages, along with the aunts and uncles. It was a great time, and we had some great memories. As a youth, I also fondly remember days with my grandma Hedrick and her fried chicken all the way from chicken coup to the fryer to my stomach. Mmm. Mmm. Good. As I grew a little bit older and became a teenager, we had this group of best friends, and you could count on them for Sunday afternoon football or Sunday afternoon basketball. It was like clockwork. We were so close and even keep in touch to this day. We even had a nickname. We called ourselves the Milroy Mafia because we were so cool and so close, and we would take care of each other no matter what. If our parents ever called into the house, we had a code.

You wouldn't rat me out. I wouldn't rat you out.

Relationships matter. In fact, recently, one of my cousins, even though he's a bit younger than I am, called me and said, "Hey, I'm coming to Dallas on Sunday. You want to hang out?" Boom, we hung out and watched a little March Madness on TV and just caught up. I can go back to Indiana almost any weekend if I choose, make a phone call and one of those guys, if not more, would be immediately available to have a cold beer.

Friendships Matter

Relationships are very important in life, but I think the best relationships that I have are ones that are long lasting. These are more than just our best friends and our cousins. I think about my relationship with Purdue University and the many people I know from college many years later. We often get a degree and move on. I've taken a different path on my relationship with my alma mater. I am a sports junkie. I follow every sport including men's diving as we create NCAA champions and Olympic medalists. Basketball and football top my list. But also included are volleyball, track and field, and more. I am passionate about athletics. I am also an annual donor of reasonable proportions to both engineering and athletics. I go back and I speak to students, from industrial engineering students to even the aviation students. And to be clear, Purdue sports are great, but also bring heartbreak. My little brother Jeff and I live and die together in those moment of victory and defeat.

When I think about relationships, it's not just about my cousins and my friends. It's about the university that I hold dear, who gave me an education that gave me the life I currently enjoy. I want to give back to that relationship and have over the last 30 plus years, including writing articles for the engineering magazine. I think about my relationship with other organizations, like Junior Achievement, where I spent ten years on the board of directors and was even the chairman of the board. These commitments helped to form very special lifelong relationships.

Even though I'm no longer on the board, but just a couple of months ago, I received a call from them. It's the hundredth-year anniversary of Junior Achievement, and they said, "Mark, I know you still have a relationship with us. You are still a regular donor. Would you be more involved in 2019 as we celebrate the hundredth anniversary of Junior Achievement?" That was an easy answer for me to say, "Yes! Tell me how I can help celebrate a hundred years of Junior Achievement to further the mission."

It goes back to this: If the relationship is at the right level, there's really nothing that's too hard in the workplace to work through. My current boss, Cornelius, asked me recently why I didn't take the exit package that American offered last year. He knew my age; he knew of some of my frustrations with the company. It didn't take me long to answer him. One of the reasons I didn't leave was I needed to be here because of the relationships I had with my team.

A strong part of my job was to protect them through this company reorganization. I valued the relationships with them, and I promised them I wouldn't leave during a time of imbalance. I felt like I owed them that in exchange for their time and loyalty and certainly performance. It was time to "circle the wagons" around my team to make sure that they were protected through this company reorganization and downsizing.

Hey, there were other reasons that were more selfish, but that was the number one reason why I didn't walk away—because of the relationships that I have with my team. I value them so much. Relationships matter.

I was very lucky when I think back to all the places I've lived—from Indiana to Dallas, Texas, to Oyster Bay, New York, and then to Valencia, California. In every place, there was always a handful of people who played significant roles in my life.

I didn't go to New York for four years then just walk away. I didn't go off to California to just leave everything behind. I have strong relationships there that are still important to this day. I know people in each place such that if I go to those cities—or when I know that they're having a life event, a birthday, or anniversary—I'll be a part of it. That's how close we are. We're always going to stay connected, and if something's going on in their lives or my life, or if someone needs someone to talk to, they are the best friends who will be there forever. The ones who have my back. They are the ones I'll circle the wagons and plead the fifth for. Do you make an impact on the people you know and places you've been?

I've been blessed, but I think it works both ways. Relationships are hard. If you realized how much relationships matter, and how they can change your life, it's never too late. Your life will be much easier and richer.

It's amazing how relationships get better because of golf. To be accurate, to build a relationship that works, you must be in partnership with others. It can't just be one-way. On any given weekend, if you want to play a round of golf, and with some cold beer, you can always find the four of us needed for a round. Sure, it's golf, but that's just the thing that connects people. You've got to find something, a connection that everyone can have together and then do that! You must meet people in their world, whether it's via sports or love or the cold beer or the fun activity or the country music concert. Whatever that connection is, if you can find a way to connect with people, the relationship changes in so many good ways.

When conflict in any relationship occurs, I go back to reminding myself that the relationship—the only relationship I have in this world—that's going to complete me, that will make me truly happy, is with God Himself.

When I put that relationship with my heavenly Father into perspective, it helps to make me find a path forward with all the relationships I have on planet earth. Life is a gift, but so are the relationships we are given.

Years ago, I bought a King Arthur sword. Yes, a real-life replica, and it's pretty cool. I bought it because to me it symbolized three things in life that really mattered to me:

- Friendship

- Equality

- Inclusion

You know Knights of the Round Table. One for all, all for one. Each time I look at it, I smile for the meaning and symbolism it has to me. I think that epitomizes the fundamentals of relationships right there.

Key Takeaways and Insights #8

Relationships Matter

- How does this apply to you?

- What learning can you take away?

- Relationships matter and take work to maintain in a healthy way for both parties
- The proper perspective can really help!
- Do you value your relationships over the negative events that occur in them?
- Do you practice forgiveness in your relationships?
- Do you first seek to understand intent when conflicts arise?

Parenting

This chapter is about choosing love over criticism; shaping your kids through different seasons—like divorce, hormones, and college choices—while leading, not ordering; giving them the space to make their own decisions; and trusting through all of the life lessons, so they will know you did your best.

Parenting is a labor of love. If you're a parent, you understand how important it is to be intentional. And by the way, anytime someone wants to talk about parenting, I immediately feel overwhelmed by the magnitude of the topic. No one is an expert! You've got to do the best that you can. But I'll give you my version of my own parenting style and thoughts. Take what you will from my own journey.

Starting with the Heart

Parenting must start with a loving and forgiving heart, right? A big difference in parenting style was probably one of the major conflicts in my first marriage. That's because we are all unique and different people come from different perspectives. Everyone parents differently. What you do is not what your friends do. But I believe the very best parents begin with a loving heart.

My personal notions about the heart of a parent is one that delivers a lot more hugs than it does scolding or discipline. All the attributes of love that we've talked about—unconditional love, sacrificial love, and forgiving love—are the obvious components of a heart that demonstrates love. A love that is there to be able to not just break up the fight, stop the argument, or stop the temper tantrum, but also be able to find the right moment, when calm has been achieved, to take advantage of the teaching moment.

Be willing to learn from your kids. Being a student of the lessons your children can teach you about the world around you. It will go a long way in developing healthy trust and giving your kids the creative space to figure things out. I think the heart of a loving parent who's willing to teach and capable of teaching starts with those three attributes of love, which I think are very critical, very important, very fundamental to achieving the parenting style. To be clear, I've learned plenty from Makayla and Mallory!

People often say, "If you want to be a good parent, you must read all the most recent books on child-rearing." We know that professionals may know a thing or two about what works and what doesn't, but I am sure if you are a parent, you know that there is no book out there that can prepare you for life with your unique children. Books can help, but the way you parent (or try to parent) is as much framed by how you prepare for it and how you grew up. No, that doesn't mean you have to repeat how you were raised; it simply means, whether we had a good or bad example, we take away from our childhood and bring it with us in our parenting.

My parents loved us, hugged us, and truly poured into us, not only through prayer but by teaching us those critical life lessons as we were growing up. The mother of my children was raised very differently than I was. From my observations through the years before (and even after) our divorce, I can see that her parents were strict, authoritative, and willing to ground and scold. It was not in line with how I felt our daughters should be raised.

I was fortunate years ago to be gifted a book that truly opened my eyes to the value of my role as a father to daughters. I've read it a couple of times and gifted it to others a couple of times. What was the book? *Strong Fathers, Strong Daughters* by Meg Meeker.

So many people forget that the role of a father in raising children, and for me raising amazing daughters, is that you are a role model. It's the role model that will influence the type of husband, the type of men, that my daughters may want to choose to be married to down the road. The moment you realize how you model parenthood and marriage—and in my case, fatherhood—you realize that you are truly a role model and they are watching you. Think about all your own personal actions and what is the right reaction in the moment of tantrum or disagreement. Maybe your child says or does something that's just stupid because they're immature. Your immediate reaction changes when you stop and think that you are a role model. When you think about it, what are you modeling? I know I'm modeling behavior, character, and so much more for Makayla and Mallory every day.

Being a Role Model

You never know who is watching you, and the truth is,

you may never know how many times your behavior changed someone's life for better or worse. Many kids look at their parents as one of the role models they may choose to emulate in the future.

You may not choose to be, but like it or not, you are a role model.

For me, my parents shaped me and how I would grow up to interact, not only with my own kids but the teams that I would lead. They would tend to listen to me and let me have a voice in the conversation. In a moment of stress or strife, there'd be a hug more often than a grounding or a scolding. Those were the tools they gave me to carry on into my own parenting journey. I know I made my mom cry on more than one occasion. Maybe the behavior I was demonstrating at the time was disrespectful. There was a moment where, whether I knew it right then or I figured it out later—and certainly after years of life—that she was teaching me something. She was teaching me about patience and what true love is.

As a parent, you get to choose how you respond. If you are working through a disagreement or a conflict, there is a moment when you have to decide if it is more important to be the only winner, or find your way to work through things to an ending that is a win-win for everybody. Why is that important? There are many parents, and people for that matter, who always must win. It doesn't matter the argument or the damage done by winning. As a parent, you actually get to win by default. But the big question is, at what cost? What do you truly get out of winning? What did you lose?

It's a different kind of philosophy. You can start from a place of sovereign authority, or you can let your child have his or her voice.

For me, in the moment of disagreement, my goal was to try to calm down and reflect. There was going to be a different outcome if I didn't respond appropriately in the heat of the moment with, "You're grounded!" Later, after there's calm and we've walked through things, then I can respond in love but still in authority, "You're losing your cell phone for the next ten days." You have a choice to respond in anger and lose the teaching moment—or to stop, react with calm, digest what happened, and create a thoughtful teaching moment about what happened and how you could do something differently next time.

I can hear you now, *Sure, that sounds easy on paper, Mark, but when you are angry it is not so easy.* It's not easy; in fact, it is downright hard.

Work-Life Separation

Leading at work can be just as complicated as parenting at home. Often it is hard to separate parenting and teaching your kids from leading and coaching at work. It isn't two separate forms of leadership for me, and I would be shocked if too many people said they have different styles that they can turn on and off for work and for home. Being authentic means you are the same no matter where you are. Me, I'm the same person at home as I am at work. You're getting the authentic me, the same me at work and at home. To me, it is easier to be authentic and be just me no matter where I am than it is to be two different people. It is fascinating that there are people who think they can shut certain things off for home and work. We are who we are, all the time. You can paint a zebra black, but underneath, it still has stripes. Why not be who you are all the time?

Lessons and Trust

When you look back at your kids, once they roll that car down the driveway to college, and you see the lessons from teaching them how to drive and trusting them to make choices. You want to know you gave them as many lessons and as many good habits as possible. When it was time for Makayla to roll down the driveway, she came to me and said she wasn't sure she wanted to go to college right away. I knew this had to be her decision. I knew from her personality she had to make the choice on her own.

I had set it up to pay for both girls to go to college. That didn't mean I was going to give her the college money to not go. I created a spreadsheet to lay out what her finances would look like both in and out of college. "This is your budget for both: if you're not in college, and if you are. These are the bills I'm paying while you are in college, and these are being paid for by you because you're an adult, making the adult decision to be on your own and not in school." This was a teaching moment. Nothing in life comes free, not even when you want to support your kids through college. Shortly after that, she came back to me with the commitment to start with community college. If you know your kids and you're teaching them every day, you will be able to give them a chance to realize they can be trusted to make decisions. When you give them the tools, they can make choices that you can trust. By the way, Makayla now holds a degree in psychology from the University of North Texas! And she's discussing the potential master's degree journey. Mallory, my youngest, is also well on her way in her junior year at Tarleton State University.

Your parenting leadership and business leadership are

directly related. In both, we are using some of the same techniques we used in parenting leadership when we're leading people in business.

For raising children and for teams in business, your biggest hurdle—and the biggest thing you can do to empower both—is to not do their work. When you trust them and when you work to hire the right people, you can give them the right guidance and trust them to do things. When you give people trust and empowerment, to both your children and your coworkers on your team, they will give you something extra when they realize that you placed trust in them. That builds confidence to go do this task or to go do that job.

Teaching moments happen in the home and at work. It is the decision to use those moments without leaving a wake of bodies behind you that will truly show how well you are leading.

It's a parent and a leader's job at home and work to put boundaries around the people you have responsibility for and position them for success. The most important role a leader has is to create the environment where success is inevitable.

Parenting is about success and leadership.

When your children are small, it's all about protection. As they get older, it's about leadership.

Adaptability is a key to being both a leader in the workforce and a successful leader as a parent. Many parents don't view their role as parents as leadership, but it is. Being an adaptable leader is important.

What does adaptability mean? It means you must be the one to adapt. It's not all about you. It means that by practicing adaptability, just because one thing might work today in that meeting doesn't mean will work tomorrow in the other meeting. It's the same with parenting.

As much as you need to be adaptable, make sure you know your audience and understand that you must know who they are and adapt your style to produce the best results. It's the same way with your children.

People go through different stages and growth periods. How can you adapt your leadership and parenting style? Your resiliency in business and as a parent are what that will help you persevere during challenging times. There are skills that are transferable in parenting and leadership. Your children will travel their own journey of life just like we do, and it's easy to be focused on our own stuff. They've got pain, victory, needs, and joys to talk about too. We can't get lost in our own stuff. When my girls needed someone to talk to other than me, my mother and my father were always there for them. They knew that Grandma would answer the phone, would always be someone that would be there to listen, to console. Surround your kids with mentors and leaders from all walks of life. It takes a village. Don't let anybody tell you otherwise.

Time spent with your children matters too. I treasure the time I have spent going to dinner and hanging out with my girls. Special memories have been made going to music concerts, sporting events, visiting national parks, and traveling to places such as the Kentucky Derby. There was also that day in Tennessee at the Banana Pudding Festival!

The heart of a parent is one that delivers a lot more hugs than it does scolding or discipline. Parenting is not unlike leadership. Both require you to be a strong and confident leader, but the magic happens when you can do it with calm and love too.

Key Takeaways and Insights #9

Parenting

• How does this apply to you?

• What learning can you take away?

• Raising a family takes a team, so lead with intention.
• What is your parenting style?
• Do your children have a voice in things?
• Are you adapting your style as your children grow and mature?
• Do you adapt your style based on the situation at hand?
• Do you shower your children with love and hugs?

Dignity
and
Leadership

Express Dignity

This Insight offers that dignity is the cornerstone of all people interactions.

One of the lessons added I try to live by is to express dignity in all interactions. It's an important insight because a lot of people live with emotions that cause them to feel shame or act as if they have lost their dignity. Partnerships and relationships center on human dignity. In fact, it is the cornerstone of all human relationships. A lot of other words come to life when I think about dignity. Words like respect, understanding, inclusion, equality, and love. If we are recognized for who we are, our identity will pull all those words together—all those characteristics are summed up in who we were created to be. Human dignity is how you interact with other people and how you treat them. If you're treated with dignity, you'll be included in conversations or decisions. As a leader, if you treat people like that, you will ignite them to be their best, to offer their genuine self, and to participate.

What is dignity lived out in reality?

Dignity is all about showing others that they matter, no matter what their life status. It's about respecting and understanding that we all just want a safe place in life.

Dignity is showing kindness to a homeless man. It's showing love to someone who doesn't benefit you. It's common for each of us to express love to those who are helping us personally or professionally. But dignity doesn't discriminate, and it recognizes that everyone has a unique perspective and brings value.

Back in 2001, I oversaw LaGuardia Airport. When the Twin Towers fell on September 11, I realized that many people were looking to me to tell them what was going on and that their jobs would be safe.

I realize now, years later, that what those people wanted to know was that someone cared, understood what they were going through, and was willing to help.

They needed to be reassured that we would be there for them, and that they would still be able to care for their families. It was a time of great uncertainty, and our people needed to feel safe under our leadership and working for American Airlines.

All my leadership experience came together in one moment of truth. I remember standing on break room tables where employees gathered and just talking to them. More importantly, I listened to them express their fears and concerns. It was all about treating them with dignity and respect when they needed it the most.

Years later, and in the aftermath of all that had happened, I began working with Donna Hicks, an organizational psychologist with Harvard University and the Overland Resource Group. The Overland Resource Group, or ORG, is a consulting firm based in Kansas. Donna's work in resolving conflict through mutual respect and dignity is legendary. She had worked with Nelson Mandela during the time of South African apartheid, as well as the IRA and police in Northern Ireland.

Donna took us on a journey that opened my eyes to the challenges we were facing at American Airlines. These challenges were a result of dignity violations that came about through years of joint collective bargaining agreements, executive compensation, and even the events of 9/11. The violations had occurred unintentionally, but they had to be addressed if we were to move forward. With the help of Donna and the ORG team, we were able to begin the healing process and move forward as a company. A key component was a deeper understanding of how much dignity means to people.

What we learned during the next two years with Donna can be illustrated by describing seven levers of employee commitment around human dignity.

A lever is something you push that helps you move something. Like a gas pedal is a lever to accelerate the car, there are levers that can accelerate a leader or a person in life. You can push these levers thoughtfully and intentionally and bring about change in your business and relationships. When you think of your own organization, what kind of employee experience do you want to create? As a leader, understanding how to use these seven levers to guide your people and create positive outcomes is crucial. It's all based on a foundation of human dignity.

1. Inclusion and Recognition

Do I feel included in my company? Does my voice matter?

Am I respected? Am I appreciated and recognized for the good work that I do? Do my peers and my supervisor recognize me as a human being? Do they know what I'm going through? These are the questions that are in the minds of your people. Employee recognition is the transformative force that is needed to build a culture of inclusion. You must engage all your employees and help them feel understood and appreciated. Dignity is rooted in trust and respect. Letting your employees know they are valued, that their contributions matter, and their voices are heard will help create a sustainable culture of inclusion and recognition.

2. Job Design and Work Environment

Each role or job in your company should be intentionally designed so that success is inevitable. Provide all the adequate training, equipment, and support that is necessary for someone to be effective in their role within the company. Create a system or culture that allows feedback and have processes in place that makes it easy for your people to have a voice. When people have all the necessary tools they need to succeed, they will perform at a higher level, provided the right person is in the right role. Empowering your people and giving them autonomy demonstrates your trust and respect. Too often leaders describe a job and how to do it but fail to communicate the "why" behind it. Help your people understand the significance of their role and its connection to the bigger picture.

3. Interaction with Leadership

These interactions are a two-way street. A supervisor needs to respect the opinions and professional competence of their people. Conversely, employees should respect the competence and opinions of their supervisor. It's about mutual respect and a team mindset. It's working together jointly to create solutions and achieve objectives. It's important to understand that all culture is local, meaning it comes down to how people are interacting with each other at every level of your business. For example, if my management team in Los Angeles is behaving differently than my team in Tucson or Phoenix, then the desired outcome may be impacted in a negative way. It will also impact the way employees feel about the company, as well as the kind of experiences your customers have with your business. It always comes back to everyone treating others with dignity and mutual respect.

4. Empowerment

I touched on empowerment earlier when talking about work environment and job design. When employees do not feel empowered, they will administer company policies in a legalistic, black-and-white manner. What follows is that the experience of your customers will be the same. Instead of conversing with your customers, employees would simply state, "This is our policy" and move along to the next person. It creates interactions that are cold and lifeless. An empowered employee creates solutions on their own and therefore becomes invested in the outcome. This behavior creates an entirely different experience for your customers. Instead of feeling like a meaningless number, they come away from the interaction feeling as though they matter and your company cares.

Naturally, empowerment has boundaries. Employees cannot be empowered to give away a million dollars, but they should have options available to them and know they can use them at their discretion. When your employees realize they have options in which to manage and help customers, you create an environment where your employees deliver the best customer service possible.

5. Process Fairness around Company Policies and Procedures

Does your company have policies and procedures in place that are understood by your employees and that will help create positive outcomes? Do you have an appeal process through which employees can be heard? There are always other employees observing how you deal with other employees, so the way in which you administer your policies is important. Having a process doesn't always mean equal outcomes, but can lead to a decision being made that is best for all concerned parties. We're talking about process fairness, not outcome fairness, which is the next lever.

6. Outcome Fairness

Are the decisions you make regarding your employees perceived as being fair? For example, at an American Airlines boarding gate in LaGuardia, I may have assigned two people to work, but in Los Angeles I have four. This could be perceived as being unfair to the employees in LaGuardia. It's important to weigh each decision and policy and ensure it is fair across the entire company.

The same concept should be applied to organizational rewards and compensation programs. Are they fairly implemented and distributed throughout the company? Do all employees have a fair shot at development opportunities and promotions?

When process fairness is married to outcome fairness, you send a powerful message to your people. They will feel like the company is treating them well.

7. Organizational Membership

There's a reason why churches are relevant today and why families love to connect with each other. There's a reason why people join clubs, charities, or fraternities. The reason is that people want to feel like they are a part of something bigger than themselves. What you want to do in your company is create an environment where people feel like they are a part of something larger than just their particular role. At American Airlines, I want the person working a gate at DFW to know they are more than just a gate agent. I want them to know that what they are doing is crucial to the success of the entire company, and I want them to stay with the company for a long time.

Recently, American Airlines went through a major initiative to define our purpose. It's more difficult than you may realize to concretely define why your company exists. Our goal was to define why we were in business and to pinpoint our "why"? Our purpose is to care for people on life's journey. We want to care for those who work for American Airlines. Whether it's a layoff, a death in their family, or some other hardship, we will be there for them.

It's also about caring for our customers who fly with us. It's about more than merely transporting them from Dallas to Orlando. It means helping them get to another city where they can attend an important business conference or spend time with family members they don't often see.

The most amazing thing about the process of defining our purpose was the way in which we did it; we didn't start from the top down. Instead, we brought in 130 frontline employees to attend a three-day workshop to discuss the reason why we were in business. We put together a series of activities to help people understand the purpose behind what we do as a company. Once our purpose was defined and understood, people could begin to see how they fit in and how their contribution was important.

People could feel that they were not working for American Airlines just for the money, but for the greater purpose of caring for each other and caring for our customers. It really changed their view of the company, and they are more apt to focus their energy on creating positive results. They understood that they were a part of something bigger. How do you think that made them feel about American Airlines? They were proud to be a part of the organization, and people who are proud of the company they work for will recommend that company to others. When you see this happening, you know you have created a powerful feeling of unity and belonging.

I've worked hard for more than a decade to bring these seven levers to life, and they are unbelievably powerful. When you have a leadership team that can apply these, the results are staggering. We recently surveyed 130,000 global team members, and within my HR Shared Services team, we had a 91 percent engagement score. That means that 91 percent of our team members are either engaged or highly engaged with my team at American Airlines and the work that we do. That's just one example of what can happen when you apply these seven levers thoughtfully, recognize human dignity, and create an environment where people can succeed.

The way in which you interact with people means everything. Understanding and respecting different points of view is crucial and becomes especially important in times of conflict. Most people don't intend to inflict negative outcomes on their peers, children, or bosses. But the way you think about human dignity, and the feelings that are behind the way people act and feel, will change things. You can shift an entire conversation by seeking clarity and understanding.

It's been a journey of several stops and starts for American Airlines over the last several years, but we're gaining a lot of traction. Everyone has an awareness of what it can do for the company if we look for ways to use the seven levers of dignity.

For example, in our early journey we gave our leadership a series of litmus questions that the CEO and the senior leaders of the company can use when making decisions for the company. There are intended consequences for every decision. If I want to build an airplane that has more seats in it to drive revenue, there are all kinds of conscious and intentional decisions that must take place. What we did was provided a template of questions for leaders to simply be more introspective on their decisions. When a decision is made, be sure to ask, What groups are most affected by the decision and how are they likely to view the decision? What were the specific impact of this decision? The answers to these questions may or may not change the decision, but what it can do is change how you educate and communicate. It may change how you implement the decision, or it may actually change the decision itself. The questions were put in place to help leaders think differently about the decisions in order to create an environment that reflects understanding and dignity. It's one way in which we implement the seven levers. And it puts it into the seven levers more thoughtfully. What happened in the first part of our journey with Donna Hicks and the Overland Resource Group is we gained a lot of momentum. Then came the bankruptcy and leaders got distracted by the restructuring of the company. We had a whole set of new leaders to educate. Some of the components are in place, and it's not as holistic of approach I would like to see, but things are headed in the right direction.

We are using the levers and are really pushing inclusion or recognition. We have the most robust recognition program at American Airlines that I've seen in 30 plus years. People are using it and using recognition to drive results.

Over time, we will work hard to pull it together.

Donna Hicks recently released her latest book, entitled Leading with Dignity. I purchased copies for all my People team leaders at American Airlines. My hope is that they will read it, implement the principles it contains, and start a kind of grassroots movement within the company that will spread to every person.

I've learned that many companies want to treat everybody the same. They put everyone into categories and tell them to use the Golden Rule: Treat people the way you want to be treated. But everyone is different, and treating everyone based on your likes and dislikes may not be appropriate. It's more about applying the Platinum Rule: Treat people the way they want to be treated.

One of the issues I noticed at American Airlines is that our senior leaders were not getting out and talking to our people. They didn't know them, which made respect and feelings of inclusion more difficult. This in turn affects perception, and many frontline employees were complaining that their leaders were drawing huge salaries but never bothered to come out into the field.

In the late 2000s, we had a steering committee of the CIO, the CFO, the senior VP of airports, and CMO. We had five of the most senior leaders of the company. We said to them, "Hey, we're going to create this really cool thing called the Customer Cup, and every quarter we're going to recognize five cities for doing great work in customer experience for improving results. What we want you to do is take one day out of the quarter and fly to the winning city. Each of you will take a Customer Cup and go to the city for a day. We'll order cakes and tell them you're coming. You'll take the Cup and walk around thanking people for their efforts."

By doing this, senior leaders were getting to know the people working the front lines in Tucson, Guatemala, Mexico City, and New York. The result is that respect and inclusion harpoon naturally, and the people on the frontlines feel like they matter.

Your culture is a compilation of the stories that people tell about your company. In 2007 and 2008, the stories people were telling at American Airlines all had to do with 9/11, layoffs, and restructuring. By starting the Customer Cup program, we were able to begin changing the story. We're working to intentionally create new stories and become aware of how we treat people and interact with them. This is another way in which we implement the seven levers of dignity.

I remember walking through the airports for my first time in 1991. I was learning the airports, as well as the company's policies and procedures. There was so much I didn't know, yet I was supposed to be the expert. Every day I was the

Manager on Duty. At most every gate, an agent or supervisor would come to me and say, "Hey, Mark, I have a problem." And I would say, "Tell me about the problem." Once I understood what the problem was, the first question I would ask was, "What do you think we should do?" It's remarkable how empowering those words are and the impact they had on the people I was interacting with. To this day, I can't think of any issue we didn't resolve, and it helped me to learn a lot at the same time. I bet it was 90 percent of the time when I simply said to them, "That's a good idea. Go try that," or, "Why don't you go do that?" By simply asking them what they thought the solution would be, I was demonstrating that I recognized the value and contribution. I showed them dignity.

When someone comes to you with a problem, they often have an idea on how to solve it. They either don't trust themselves, or they are ensuring what's within the company's boundaries. When you empower them to offer up their ideas, you are including them in the process, and they feel they're a part of the solution. You will be showing them dignity.

Key Takeaways and Insights #10

Express Dignity

- How does this apply to you?

- What learning can you take away?

- Why is it important to treat everyone with dignity?
- Dignity is the cornerstone of all human relationships. What can we do to show others they matter?
- The Seven Levers of Employee Commitment can be pushed thoughtfully and intentionally
    1. Inclusion and Recognition
    2. Job Design and Work Environment
    3. Interaction with Leadership
    4. Empowerment
    5. Process Fairness around Company Policies and Procedures
    6. Outcome Fairness
    7. Organizational Membership

Be a Good Partner

*This Insight demonstrates the value of partnerships is
important in all our interactions with the world.*

Learning to be a good partner takes the concepts from the
Insight #8 to a deeper, more focused level. Partnerships come
in a variety of shapes and sizes. When I think of partnerships,
business connections come to mind. Of course, any self-im-
provement work you do in your personal world with your
partners (family and friends) will carry over into your professional growth. It's all tied together.

Recently during a golf game, with both SAP and American
Airlines colleagues, we had some lively conversation about
partners. It's fascinating what you learn about people through
conversations like these—when you think about people as
partners rather than just as vendors, software providers, or
whatever your business connection is. Being a good partner
starts with knowing and understanding what makes your
counterpart tick, which, of course, will put your business
relationship in a better place. When you think about your

business relationships as a journey you are taking together, they will grow.

I want to illustrate this from a practical business approach before I get into the biblical part of it. When I think about partnerships, I think about creating scenarios where both parties win. I know it's important for my company to be successful, but I think we can be more successful if my partners (in this case, SAP, IBM, and Deloitte) are also successful during our journey. I make understanding what's important to them a priority for me and my team. At the same time, I'm driving to share with them what my team is all about, what we are trying to achieve, and what's important to American Airlines. I always think win-win. How do you create win-win scenarios as a starting point in all you do?

I try to build relationships in the business world, both with internal colleagues and with my partner companies, by focusing always on how I can improve in serving them. I know that I can serve them best by understanding their agenda and helping them to create wins. The more that I'm able to make them feel good, the more they're going to be interested and willing to do what it takes to create wins for my company. I always enter into new partnerships thinking about the end result—the win-win. This also goes for my work internally at American Airlines. I look for the critical partnerships we need to be successful internally. For example, my role in the company today is split among several key areas of HR Shared Services as well as strong partnerships with the employee technology and payroll leaders. It would be easy to get isolated and focused on my agenda. What I've discovered is that the more we become team players, the more we increase our chances of achieving everyone's goals. You may have heard the expression, "There's no sports team on the planet that spells T-E-A-M with an *I!*" Being a team is always about "we."

How do we think about being team players? How do we then collaborate? How do we ensure we're creating an inclusive environment where everyone's voice matters? How do we drive that forward by bringing the right people who are diverse thinkers to the table? All these questions are fundamental to how I think about creating a partnership, sustaining each other's agendas, and creating partnerships that are integrated, valued, and successful. This is essential.

We have a long-lasting partnership with Deloitte, the consulting company. Our partnership together is based on and starts with people. First, the people you bring to the table must be good, talented people with good intentions. Second, these people must establish a relationship to drive the program forward. We must all understand our roles and responsibilities. We must create a way to work things out when things get tough. Finally, trust must be present. You must be able to trust the people, trust that they know their roles, and trust that they will do their job. You also must trust that their intentions are as good as yours.

Partnering in business is like any team sport, and any worthwhile endeavor requires tremendous focus, attention, and skill. Consider it like a football team where each player has specific skill sets that are needed to execute the various plays during the game. All the players vary in size, speed, and strength. Most often they are specialists in their position and may only know what is being asked of them to execute a given play. For example, an offensive lineman may not know the route the receivers are asked to run on a given play. He does know however how to block his player. The receiver must trust the other players to do their job as best as they can. Within the team, relationships are also key. It is next to impossible for a team to be exceptional if there is constant infighting and bickering.

When you get it right—the right people, relationships, and trust—you realize you all jumped into the same pool and you all jump into the solution together. When the going gets tough, we don't want people running away from the fire. We want them running to the fire to help put the fire out and to help solve the problem. We want them locking arms and running to the fire together. This is simply another way of saying "circle the wagons" discussed in a previous Insight. That's the kind of culture to strive for.

Recently, I helped a friend write a persuasive essay. Her paper questioned whether it was better to be someone who was a big dreamer that wants to change the whole world or a practical planner that wants to accomplish smaller goals and just achieve things that were still good. She mapped out her two positions. As we were talking, I told her the idea of having a big dream and creating change in the world is great, but it can't happen in a vacuum. One person cannot do anything without others. For example, if you were a recluse in your house and ordered all your needs online and had a successful work-from-home business, you would still have to depend on customers or clients to pay you. You must depend on Amazon or some other food delivery service to bring you things. We all must depend on others.

It becomes a symbiotic dependency. After four years of working with Deloitte on many key business initiatives and some of the business services they're providing to American, we have created interdependency and a deep, dynamic relationship. Deloitte has helped us create business success in HR and payroll transformation. They have helped us set up a data privacy office and be compliant with the new global regulations for data privacy. They are a global company so what we do in return is fly their people with American Airlines more and more. So American not only is winning in the space of business transformation and business activities, but we are winning by having a greater revenue stream come to American through this partnership.

Deloitte is getting tons of revenue from American, but that doesn't serve as the real value of the partnership. We're growing the partnership in ways that are incredibly important to both companies. We need people to fly American, but we also need customers who are on business travel to fly American and buy first class or business class because those are premium seats. When we sell those premium seats, we can make a disproportionate amount of profit. It's a perfect win-win.

When people are in business with other people, we make mistakes, we make decisions, we make judgments, and things happen that are not part of the plan. From the biblical perspective, this is when we need to think about things like mercy over judgment. If you're more focused on mercy and forgiveness, you are less focused on judging people. You're willing to then forgive them and understand their true intentions and find a path forward together. When this is your mindset, partnerships survive over longer periods of time.

Mercy and forgiveness are as applicable in the business world as they are in the personal world. These are essential in creating a peaceful world and for building good relationships, including your relationship with God. When I think about the importance of bringing new voices to the table in the terms of diversity and inclusion, I think of the biblical concept of tolerance—tolerance of others and how they are different than you are demonstrated through mercy, inclusion, and love. Forgiveness is necessary for tolerance to be possible. In the business world, if all I do is hire people like me, I get no other perspective—nothing other than me. As a leader who is in search of all the best ideas and all the creativity possible, I don't want that. I want different people because the power of "we" more powerful than the power of "me."

If we don't have any base, no concrete foundation with aligned principles how are we going to maintain a partnership? Things go wrong. That's a given. It's during these times, when things aren't going as planned, that you need both unconditional and sacrificial love. When you apply these biblical principles in the business world to partnerships, you'll enjoy a high level of success. Unconditional love manifests itself in a partnership through trust in the relationship. What you're willing to do for the other party is relevant. Sacrifice is part of the partnership too. I will do things for you to help you be successful without fully expecting a payoff of some type.

There are many principles in the Bible that are applicable to business, but you can't make religion a dominant part in the workforce because it can be uncomfortable for some. But you can still live it and apply the principles in your dealings with people at work. You can show by example.

When the best of you comes out for all to see, you begin to realize how valuable different perspectives are when you're bringing people together to solve bigger problems. If I bring my authentic Mark Mitchell, it reveals the fact that Mark is also a passionate disciple of Jesus Christ. It also can reveal that someone is a Muslim who practices Islam or a person who practices Judaism or someone who's from the Indian community. When you're asking people to commit to a company, we need the diversity of many perspectives. Why does American Airlines exist? What is our mission? Simply said, American Airlines exists to care for people on their life's journey. That's broader than just flying airplanes. And when you're asking people to commit to the company, the best way to do that is to acknowledge your personal why, who you are. That's diversity and inclusion at its finest.

There is so much growth that can happen when you allow each person to be who they authentically are all the time. Successful companies build partnerships with their employees. They also partner with their business to business clients. Fundamentally, these are partnerships with people, a people relationship that goes into the business world. Everyone on the planet has discretionary energy. What do they do with that discretionary energy? When a company wants to achieve greatness, it invites you to be the best you at work. What happens is that engagement, that partnership the company's created with you, leaves you wanting to commit your discretionary energy to help the company achieve its goals.

Every year, especially during budget time, we always talk about ways to apply more toward the objectives of American Airlines. This usually means implementing ways to increase productivity. Doing this across the organization drives our business results. What I learned is that if I get more of your discretionary energy, it produces huge wins. For example, an employee staying a little later during busy times means the company is getting more of that employee's discretionary time. Across the board, that's 130,000 employees bringing that discretionary energy to work in a positive way for the benefits of the company.

When I think back to all the many roles I've had in New York, Los Angeles, and in Dallas now for the third time, I realize some of the best relationships and the best business partners I have are with the business community at LaGuardia Airport, where I was the president of the LaGuardia Managers Airport Council. This team within LaGuardia Airport was responsible for the inner workings among all LaGuardia business. It was comprised of the airlines and our other business partners—local shops, bus operators, and snow removal companies—who worked together to create a superior traveler experience. Today, they remain some of my best friends on the planet. These business partnerships were initially based on win-win business scenarios. They create not just a stronger business outcome, but they grow into stronger and supportive lifelong personal relationships.

Relationships matter, and these relationships thrive when applied appropriately in the business world. A well-constructed and well-meaning partnership will drive huge positive business outcomes over the long term. Trust me on this! If there is one thing that can change your life, it is the realization to pursue a life around people, around relationships, and trust.

It's important to think about your partnerships and to invest time in knowing your audience. Each of your people in these partnerships are going to be different. They will also be unique in terms of their interests, and they will all have different passions for life. One might be a golf enthusiast; others may have kids and may not like to participate in the usual business dinners, as it takes time away from their family. If you're willing to understand each audience and how they are unique and different, you can tailor your approach to those people. Every person you lead or partner with is a different audience, and your ability to tailor your presentation and your approach to that audience will determine how strong that partnership will be.

You must know your audience. You must be reflective and introspective. How do you interact with your audience in a way that's effective?

Many people expect people to adjust to them. I think the question to ask is, Do I have the capability as an individual to understand my audience, whether I'm on the golf course, the boardroom, or in a business deal, where I can adjust my approach accordingly to get the maximum for my company and for my partner? Some people do that very well. Some people have a limited ability to change their approach, however, and their effectiveness is diminished.

The company that can't tailor their approach for partner A versus partner B will experience suboptimal results. Knowing how the relationship can be successful and knowing how the partnership can drive a win for both parties is critical.

Every partner you are working with has a story, and until you take the time to listen, you will never be able to experience their full and genuine self. If you treat people with the dignity that they're entitled to, their stories and genuine selves will be revealed. You'll be better able to work around problems. These are opportunities to get to know people, and your relationship migrates from just a transactional level to a deeper, more personal level. Taking a little time to connect and invest in your key partnerships will always pay off.

Key Takeaways and Insights #11

Be a Good Partner

- How does this apply to you?

- What learning can you take away?

- Partnerships are simply relationships in the business environment
- Partnerships are a team sport.
- How can I create a win-win?
- Mercy and forgiveness matter...professionally and personally.

Demonstrate Leadership

Demonstrating leadership (leading by example)
is a must for leaders.

How do you demonstrate leadership?

No matter what kind of leader you are, you've got to realize that leadership is an unconditional relationship. It is not domineering, nor is it one sided. The best leaders in the world are loved, open, and collaborative.

You've got to be willing to make sacrifices for the team or for the company, and you must be forgiving. There are times when you may have to overlook some mistakes.

This may not sound like the typical definition of leadership to you!

It's important as a leader for you to understand the different phases of a relationship, being aware of where you are in the journey. Most relationships start out fun and exciting, and at some point, you will make some kind of commitment. What does that relationship look like and when things get tough: Do you walk away or buckle down and recommit yourself?

In Insight #10 we talk about dignity, respect, and trust. It's important to understand how those attributes play into your effectiveness as a leader. How does a leader push the seven levers to drive people forward in their commitment to the company and deliver positive results? Communication!

My coach and friend Tony Jeary wrote a book titled *Life Is a Series of Presentations*, which means that each time you're interacting with your people at work, you're making a presentation. You must have the ability to connect and communicate your message to your audience. This is the only way you will influence and inspire your employees and is one of the most effective ways to demonstrate your leadership. It comes down to knowing the people you are serving because being a servant is the ultimate role of leadership. It's about the people and your relationship with them.

It doesn't matter if you're leading three people or three thousand, your role is the same. Servant leadership is about meeting the needs of your people. Your job is to create an environment where success is inevitable. No doubt there will be difficult times where you are tested. Lead with a servant's heart focused on God and remember that leadership isn't for the faint of heart. You may have to confront and resolve the anxiety and challenges of your people. It will be up to you to create environment conducive to success.

If I as a leader have created an environment where people respect each other, have the training, tools, and the understanding to perform well in their jobs, then I have fulfilled my task and demonstrated true leadership.

The primary attribute of the servant leader is an attitude of selflessness. You can have your own goals and aspirations; in fact, you should. The servant leader is a principle-centered leader, and the key is that you do not put your needs and desires over and above those whom you serve. It's a never-ending balancing act of fulfilling yourself and helping others experience fulfillment.

Another way through which you can demonstrate leadership is by embracing diversity and inclusion. These are terms that everyone is talking about these days. They've become buzzwords in the world of business, and for good reasons. The bottom line is that it's the right thing to do. It's about including a wide variety of people, whether it's a diversity of thought, experience, ethnicity, or gender. It also makes perfect business sense because it addresses your blind spots as a leader. No one person can know it all, so hiring a diverse group of people is wise since it will help you cover areas in which you have no knowledge or experience. You will have surrounded yourself with people who have different experiences, information, knowledge, and skills. This is the recipe for a high-performing team. You want those working under you to behave in this way, so it is crucial that you model the behaviors you wish to see in your team.

Everything up till now leads to one thing, and that is results. As the leader, you must be able to execute and deliver results for the company. In order to do this, you must provide clarity. What is the mission? What is the purpose? Once you have answered those questions, you can focus your team on the things that matter. Every day when you go to work, there are a hundred different things begging for your attention, but a leader will narrow those things down to what matters most. The next thing you must do is focus your organization on those things. To make that happen I break it down into four categories.

First, you must delegate everything. Ensure that everything that must be done has been assigned to all levels of your
business. At American Airlines, I would make sure that there
was someone in charge of baggage handling, ticket counter
management, and cash audits. I would ensure that there was
someone to take ownership of every facet of the business at
even the lowest levels.

Second, once a person has ownership of a particular area,
sit down with them and agree upon how the job is defined and
the processes that will be put in place.

The third step is to create a plan on how to implement.
What are the resources you need? What are potential barriers
and challenges? What's your timeline? Then it's about creating
ownership, defining an effective process, and creating a plan.
What that allows the leader to then do is focus less on those
individual components and focus more on the bigger picture.

The fourth step is accountability. Is the mission moving
forward? Is there a hold up in a particular area? What solutions are needed to overcome obstacles?

Ownership, processes, planning, and accountability are
the four major components that, when put into practice, will
deliver results. If you couple those four things with strategic
communications and some change management techniques,
you will create an environment that will drive your success.

A real-world example of demonstrating leadership, and
how all these concepts came together to produce a positive outcome, was when American Airlines merged with US Airways
back in December 2013. Both companies had experienced
smaller mergers, but none of this magnitude. I was asked to
lead the technology integration management office, where we
brought together 1,400 business technology applications so

that we could decide which ones were right for the company moving forward. Neither company had any experience with such an integration, so mutual respect and collaboration were essential. It was a new relationship so it was important to offer all parties the dignity and professional trust they deserved.

Since both companies were inexperienced, the diverse group of people from both airlines would become a blessing. We needed input from every possible angle. That input was crucial in helping us know who to delegate, or make "owner" of, each task. Afterward, we could develop plans and execute them.

When the merger began, there was a lot of uncertainty and fear. We had to dig deep and build a diverse team made up of the right people. That way we would have the power of many versus the power of a select few. We had to ensure that people from both airlines had a voice, and doing so demonstrated to everyone that the newly formed leadership cared about them and could always be trusted to keep their best interests in mind.

The merger of two major airlines put these principles to the test, and in the end, they were the reason it was a success.

Early in my career, I read two books that made a significant impact on the way I think. One was *In Search of Excellence* by Waterman and Peters. The other was titled *Good to Great* by Jim Collins. Both of those books helped me to build a framework from which to build my style of leadership. I've learned that there's a certain level of results in business that are acceptable, but not exceptional. What that means is that you may meet the minimum standard that was asked of you, but can you do better? You must think in terms of excellence, rather than accepting what is good. Good gets in the way of great.

True leaders don't stop at good enough, and if they know they can do better, they will do better.

Someone who demonstrates real leadership will view improvement as a continuous work and will constantly assess themselves and their organization to ensure they're operating at full potential. A leader desires to continuously improve and relentlessly execute.

The people you lead, those who are under your care, will notice your desire for excellence and will respond to it in kind. They will see how you lead them to victory after victory, taking no credit for yourself, but instead praise the team for their accomplishments. You will become their model of a great leader, and many will seek to emulate you in some way. Leaders don't just attract followers; they create other leaders.

I currently mentor eight to ten people. The interesting thing is that the mentoring doesn't end when the workday is done. I have developed relationships with these people. We discuss their personal life, family, finances, and their goals for the future. Perhaps the best demonstration of leadership is the raising up of new leaders and the ripple effects that go on for years after your role is complete.

Key Takeaways and Insights #12

Demonstrate Leadership

- How does this apply to you?

- What learning can you take away?

- What kind of leader are you?
- Four Key Execution Elements
  - Ownership
  - Process
  - Planning
  - Accountability
- Be selfless in everything, not selfish. It's not about you.

- Are you practicing servant leadership?

- Are you creating the environment where success will be inevitable with your team?

Going from Good to Great

*Good is OK, but there is a better place. Great is
that better place and how you can get there!*

I mentioned previously that the books *In Search of Excellence*
and *Good to Great* made a huge impact on me. They helped me
to shape a mindset of my own that was geared toward excellence. I don't believe in settling for the status quo when I know
that there is much more waiting for me. The way in which you
think—your mindset—will be reflected in your actions and in
the person you become.

I was in Las Vegas not too long ago, where I was part of a
keynote interview with the President of SAP SuccessFactors.
They had allocated quality time for the interview, and at the
end, I had time to answer questions. The first four or five questions were relatively easy to answer and were questions I had
prepared beforehand to answer. The last question came as a
surprise.

"Mark, before we leave today, what would you like to tell
this group of ten thousand people?"

I smiled briefly and answered without hesitation, "Don't let 'good' get in the way of becoming great."

Why settle for good when great is another option and is attainable? Achieving great things is about having the right mindset and acknowledging that there is a better place for you, your team, and even your family. Embracing that truth is life altering and will change the way you think about life.

If good gets in the way of great, then what exactly is good? I think of good as being the status quo. This is the standard for life that many readily accept as their goal. Maybe the marriage is OK, kids are getting decent grades, and the bills are being paid on time, even if there's not much money left afterward. It's "near-term horizon" thinking with little to no thought about the long term. A mindset built around excellence will never be able to accept good in place of great.

The question is, What do people with a mindset bent on achieving great things think about? First, they think beyond the near future. They deal with the present, but they plan. These are the kind of people you want to associate with. They're innovators and are the ones who disrupt aged business models.

The Amazon model is a great example. They don't just have a one-year horizon; they also have a five-year horizon. They are focused on where they're going and how they're going to get there. Amazon is always asking, "Is that place better than where we are today?"

If they had stopped and settled for good, they would have never become what they are today. Moving from good to great is a mindset shift with a different set of attributes and characteristics. Whatever you decide to do in life, you pay for it with time. Your time, and it's something you can never get back.

To strive for anything less than your best is a waste of your precious time. Your time is a commodity, a currency that you have a limited amount of, and you don't know when you're going to run out.

Here are 25 key points you can use to help evaluate whether you're focusing your energy, and spending your time on the things that matter most to take you and your team from *good to great!*

1. Create a sense of purpose around the work that you do.

2. Inspire others, through your example and behavior, to perform at their highest level.

3. Create an environment where success will be inevitable.

4. Allow your team to help take you from where you are to a better place. This is about inclusion, diversity, and trust.

5. Promote positive relationships in your company that result in the kind of collaboration you need to eliminate blind spots, get to better places, and create better solutions.

6. Encourage others to leverage their existing network and build new networks within the company or with partners. Again, this helps eliminate blind spots and leverages the power of many, which is always better than the power of one.

7. Dignity, respect, trust. Are these attributes present in your company? And how can you leverage them?

8. Do you and your company have a mindset that creates wins for others? This creates a reciprocal effect where others will want to create wins for you.

9. Your influence with others increases when you understand their agenda and what's important to them.

10. When you discover their agenda, look for ways to help them move forward. Again, this creates a reciprocal effect, and they will be more willing to listen to the needs of your team and help with your agenda.

11. Is there an environment in your company that promotes selflessness? Without this, the previous three points will be impossible.

12. Do you recognize that you have blind spots? Do you recognize that you don't know everything, and that not all the ideas you have are the best? If you have this level of self-awareness you can leverage learning opportunities, practice active listening, and build diverse teams that will help.

13. Believe that inclusion and diversity is not just the right thing to do; it has real business benefits. It's about relationships. It's about including more voices. It's about eliminating blind spots. It's about understanding that diversity isn't just a box to check off because you hired more women or minorities.

14. Do you and your company have a continuous improvement mindset? You can be the best in the business, but if you're not looking for ways to improve, you won't be for long.

15. Transparency. Being transparent is highly relevant and is necessary to do great things. Companies that are transparent are willing to confront the reality that's in front of them and be transparent about it. They will

share information with their teams and leaders to help them understand the bigger picture. Organizations who have the attribute of transparency are companies who excel in communication and innovation. They're on their way to better places.

16. Hiring and promoting individuals based on skills, not just because they're liked. Both are important and should be considered. Companies who do this are disciplined in their thinking and problem-solving processes.

17. Solid processes. Companies who have a positive approach to process fully agree on how things will get done. They have methods of deciding the best way to get things done, innovate, and continuously improve.

18. Discipline. Leaders and companies with discipline will focus on the things that matter and will not waver. They know what it takes to achieve excellence (for example, run effective meetings).

19. Pinpoint solutions. A wise leader, and company, will not waste energy focusing on a problem. They will direct their focus on finding a solution. There's no time wasted in placing blame. The solution is found and implemented.

20. Accountability. As a leader, you know creating a culture of accountability is critical. You cannot effectively delegate if there is no accountability and without individuals who "own" their area of responsibility. A company with a culture of accountability is a company who overcomes obstacles.

21. Self-awareness. This is a necessary trait for any leader,

and an important one for companies too. You need the ability to self-examine in order to improve and grow. You need to be aware of strengths and weaknesses. That way you can double down on your strengths and improve in the areas of weakness.

22. Clarity. Nothing happens until a leader brings clarity to the table. There's no room for ambiguity in the life of a leader, or a business. If there are no clear goals, and plans to achieve them, there is no growth, and everyone will suffer.

23. Value time. Time is valuable and must not be wasted on things like unnecessary meetings. If you have something of value to say, or a genuine need, then have a meeting. Otherwise allow everyone to stay on mission. If it can be handled via email, then a meeting is not necessary. When you do have a meeting, have a clear agenda, wrap it up with action items, and assignment of tasks.

24. Effective use of emails. Speaking of emails, if you don't need to copy everyone, then don't. If you must send multiple emails to get something done, it's time to pick up the phone and call. Respect others and their time.

25. Companies who are successful set goals and then establish effective success metrics to track progress. They also have accountability in place to make sure that everyone is on the same page. Be aware of, recognize, and reward successes.

That may seem like a long list, but companies who find ways to incorporate these characteristics will shift their mindset to one that seeks excellence and will stand a good chance of succeeding. Which ones are you doing well? And where is the opportunity?

Leadership isn't easy, and there may come a time when you just aren't feeling it anymore. You're human and that is perfectly normal. Everyone has off days and everyone experiences down times. The thing about being a leader is that other people are looking to you for answers and inspiration. How do you get really motivated and inspired when you might be in a bad place? For me, music and exercise work wonders. If I have a bad day and my head is full of negative thoughts, I crank up the music and go exercise. When the endorphins kick in, the stress and tension ease, and I immediately begin feeling better. If music and exercise doesn't do it for you, find something that does because you're going to need it.

As challenging as it may be to get yourself inspired, inspiring others can prove to be even more of a challenge. Inspiring others can be done in a variety of ways, your example being one. Getting your team inspired will energize them, shift their mindset, and help them perform at their full potential. Another way to get your team inspired is to create some quick wins. If you will formulate some plans that will help your team obtain a few quick victories, their energy level will go through the roof, and their confidence in you as a leader will increase exponentially. By taking these baby steps and scoring some wins for your team, you will set them up for bigger wins down the road. This is the mindset of continuous improvement. Once you create the initial wins, keep looking for the next opportunity, and then the next. You can't go from good to great if you rest on your laurels after a couple of wins. You achieve greatness by celebrating your wins, and then going for the next one. This builds momentum and prepares your team for bigger challenges.

It's not just about business. The same process can be used in your personal life. What can you do in your personal life that can help you go from good to great? How about in your relationships? Are you expanding your network and surrounding yourself with the right people? Perhaps you have some blind spots that could be revealed and overcome if you had a strong inner circle. Sometimes great advice comes from unexpected sources. Recently, my tax advisor mentioned to me that he had some ideas I may be interested in and wanted some time to present them to me. I have a wealth management team for that and didn't really want more advice. It would've been easy to be skeptical of financial advice coming from him, but if I adopted that mindset, I may have missed out on some opportunities that would've benefitted me. I decided to hear what he had to say and then weigh my options afterward. Years of leadership has taught me to remain open-minded and to be prepared to gain valuable knowledge from unexpected sources.

The importance of a leader with an open mind cannot be overemphasized. I remember a time early in my career when I went to manage LaGuardia. I didn't know anyone there and needed to find my footing and become an effective leader as quickly as possible.

My boss at DFW offered some excellent advice when she said, "When you get to LaGuardia, on your first day, get out of your car and walk to the skycaps on the curb and introduce yourself. Then go to the ticket counter and do the same thing. After that, then go through security to the gates and do the same thing, and then go to the ramp. Get to know everyone."

That little piece of advice was some of the best I have ever received. I took her advice and made my rounds throughout the airport. I made it a part of my routine and kept it going for all the years I was there. It wasn't long before I knew everyone, and they knew me. I established genuine relationships with everyone, and it all started with a simple greeting, "Good morning. Nice to see you. How's it going?"

It established a perspective in my team that said, *Oh, this new guy wants to know us and make time to talk to us.* I was approachable and interested in them personally. Another reason this was so impactful was because I was replacing a man who had been in charge there for 25 years. The former manager led from his office through his staff, and the frontline people never saw him. They all probably assumed I would behave in a similar fashion. By taking the time to develop real relationships, I was able to demonstrate from the beginning that I was different, and that I cared about them personally. One of the most meaningful things I did for the people in LaGuardia was let them know I was buying a house in one of their communities. This shifted their mindset, because they had not expected for me to put down roots and become one of them. It let them know I was looking to stay long term and enhanced my credibility.

The guys who worked in baggage handling were a little difficult and a bit more standoffish in the beginning. During my walks around I would like to stop in and say hello and try to get to know them. We would talk sports or whatever mattered to them. Then something happened that changed their view of me. Turns out that they had their own softball team, and they had heard that I had played softball on the DFW team. They called the guys at DFW to get the lowdown and heard I was pretty good. One day, out of the blue, they asked me if I was going to play on their softball team. Suddenly, I was no longer just the managing director of the airport. I was the guy that played softball, a guy they could drink a beer with and joke with on and off the softball field.

That one little thing changed their entire perspective. It made me human, it made me relatable.

I share these examples to illustrate that there's more to being leader than achieving victories and going from good to great. A leader is the servant of his or her team and must build genuine relationships with them. They must know you care, that you will lead them with integrity, and that you will lead them to better places. This is not something you will learn in MBA school. It isn't a principle or educational theory focused on in any place of higher education. It's servant leadership, and it's the path to greatness that allows you to bring everyone with you.

Key Takeaways and Insights #13

Going from Good to Great

- How does this apply to you?

- What learning can you take away?

- Are you truly giving your all in what you do?
- What can you do to go from good to great?
- Of the 25 principles offered, have you assessed where you are at each?
- Are you relatable to your team?
- Are you in a good place? Ready for *great*?

Life Balance, Inspiration and Health

Create Experiences

Stuff is great, but let's create experiences!
Choose experiences over material things.

Do you have a bucket list? To answer my own question, yes, I do. I started this process a long time ago by making a list of all the things I wanted to do before leaving earth. I keep my list in a folder, and many times, I will take the folder to meetings. This helps keep me grounded and reminds me of why I must do something that I may not like.

The list includes the same life goals as many people have, as well as experiences like parachuting from an airplane, trekking up mountains, and floating down the Amazon. But it also includes some very personal items, like joining my friends at the Masters, which I did in 2019 when I watched Tiger Woods win on that Sunday! Repeatedly I have witnessed the fragility and brevity of life. The time you are given to spend here on earth is very short, especially when compared to eternity in heaven. So why not create a bucket list to create the experiences that make you happy while you are here? Life is meant to be full of joy. Experiences that fill your soul can add to your life in ways you never imagined.

Years ago, I decided to fully understand my personality traits and strengths. I am sure you have realized that I am attracted to learning. Learning has always been high on my list of strengths. I have a natural tendency to do things that lead to learning, and that's one of the reasons I like my bucket list. I have found that these experiences have also led me to learn about other cultures, areas of the world and pursue adventure experiences. As this book is published, Gina is nearing completion of one major bucket list item, which is to visit all 193 United Nations recognized countries. Wow! Some people yearn for a new pick-up truck, a motorcycle, or a second house. My bucket list delivers learning and experiences.

I graduated from Purdue University in 1985 with a degree in industrial engineering. Like most of my graduating classmates, I jumped directly into looking for a job. I joined American Airlines as an industrial engineer, and within a few months I was working at their headquarters in Dallas. The hours were endless, and almost everyone there was committed to the company and achieving the goals set forth by the management team.

As a new employee, the typical two-week vacation was normally split up over the course of the year's worth of work. There was very little time for any bucket list adventures and travel.

Before you feel sorry for me, let me say this: I did take some amazing trips and used the free travel perk as much as anyone there. But work, the job, and my career were a high priority, and I wanted to make the most of it. I was very intentional about my travel and the things that were important to me. I recognized that

1. I'd rather spend time with you than spend money on you.

2. Experiences are learning lessons.

3. The best we can give is ourselves.

4. Making memories is important.

My bucket list also contains items that I consider stretch goals or slightly more adventurous goals. Every time I cross something off the list, I learn a little more about myself and my purpose here on earth. My accomplishments listed on my resume are what I have been hired to produce. The company, my team, and my family expect me to achieve those goals. The bucket list is outside of that. It pushes me beyond those barriers and unleashes continued relentless pursuit of the meaning of my purpose. Crossing something off the bucket list takes me a step closer to finding meaning beyond the confines of a career, secure job, and good education.

The bucket list also represents freedom. My resume highlights my responsibilities and production over the last 30 plus years. Although I had some say in these goals and responsibilities, they were given to me by the organization. I really didn't have total freedom in what was assigned to me or how I would achieve it. My bucket list is totally mine. I choose the items on it, and I assign meaning and value to them. In addition to my bucket list of the things I aspire to do, I also have a well-documented list of things I've accomplished and done. It's a reminder of the blessed life I am living.

How do you create experiences? What must you know to create experiences that will help you find meaning? Here are some of my tips.

1. We can't control time.

"Father time always wins" (Charles Barkley).

Life teaches us that we won't always get what we want right away; it teaches us that we don't have control over time no matter how good our time management skills are and no matter how good we are at predicting our future. If it's not our time yet, we can do nothing about it. Thoughtfully use and enjoy the God-given time we have each and every day. What are you doing with your time?

2. Test yourself against fear and failure.

"Success is not final; failure is not fatal: it is the courage to continue that counts" (Winston S. Churchill).

In school when we failed a class, it was easy to make up for it or study harder for the next one, but in life, failure can scar us or even change our whole perspective on the meaning of life. Life teaches us that failure is a part of it, and that success can only come after so many failures. We learn how to move on from failure and accept it as part of our journey.

3. We must face our fears.

"Don't be afraid of your fears. They're not there to scare you. They're there to let you know that something is worth it" (C. JoyBell C).

Life teaches us that at some point we will be faced with things that terrify us. We can't escape fear, so we must learn how to face it and walk with it.

4. Nothing is impossible.

"Listen to the mustn'ts, child. Listen to the don'ts. Listen to the shouldn'ts, the impossible, and the won'ts. Listen to the never haves, then listen close to me … Anything can happen, child. Anything can be" (Shel Silverstein).

Life is difficult, but it's also fascinating. In the blink of an eye, it can present us with a wonderful opportunity that can change our life around. It can bring us closer to our dream job or our dream partner. Life can make our dreams come true.

Key Takeaways and Insights #14

Create Experiences

- How does this apply to you?

- What's your key takeaway?

- Do you have a bucket list?
- What's on your bucket list, and how many items have you completed?
- Are you intentional about creating experiences?
- What are your values around the experiences you want to create?
- I encourage you to also write down the many experiences in life already accomplished, such as your wedding day, graduation, or youthful indiscretion. Here are some of mine:
  - ‣ A trip to several national parks with my girls
  - ‣ The Kentucky Derby with my girls
  - ‣ An African safari with my girls
  - ‣ Three trips to see a full solar eclipse with Gina and a trip to Antarctica
  - ‣ Boys' trip to Scotland, the home of golf
- What are yours?

Understand Balance

This Insight asks, Is it possible to achieve balance?
Let's redefine it. What does it mean to you?
What is balance?

Talking about balance in your work life and personal life is like talking about climate change or whether or not people landed on the moon. Balance feels like a myth, and everyone wants balance and believes it is important, but how to achieve it without having to give up anything is a conundrum. What makes this subject even more controversial is that balance gets redefined from generation to generation. What's even more difficult about work and life balance is that it is impacted by the culture of the organization for which you work, your values, and your personality type.

Technically, balance is the outcome, good or bad, at achieving an equilibrium between the world around us and ourselves. This balance is less about achieving an equilibrium but more like making sense out of a vortex of three currents:

1. Things we want to do (desires),

2. Things we need to do (priorities),

3. The things you should do (healthy).

All three are constant current and are forces against each other. It's like balancing while standing on a three-legged stool. Each leg represents one of the three priority currents. Balance is the outcome and the measure of your ability to create and sustain work-life balance among the three.

There is one thing that almost everyone will admit is true. Balance is mostly a function of time management. How you spend your time impacts how balanced and healthy your life is. When you think about your available resources like money, energy, and possessions, time is the only one that cannot be increased. Once time passes it cannot be added to, you cannot buy or borrow more, and it cannot be taken from anyone unless they decide to give it away. Time is your most important resource. Each person manages his or her time daily although others have input about it. One thing is certainly for sure; each daytime expires and can never be taken back.

Managing your time is also a skill like investing in the stock market or understanding complicated business formulas. Most people just don't give it much thought. Mistreating your time is something that almost all of us have done. The outcome is always the same—an unbalanced life.

First, you must determine what a balanced life definition means for you. Whether we work, go to school, or are retired, we all have responsibilities and we all desire to be effective at what we do. Although everyone's definition may be different, I think everyone would agree that a well-balanced life would encompass a couple of key concepts.

1. It would enable you to perform personally and professionally at your optimal level.

2. It would lead to peace of mind that your effectiveness and effort are the best they can be.

3. All your responsibilities and commitments could be met.

4. Because of balance, you can be healthier and happier in all areas of your life.

5. Balance is like nutrition. With no food you lose your health. You would not be effective. You would eventually die.

As a young executive with a new job at the company's headquarters, I decided to arrive early on my first day to experience the atmosphere of the office. I arrived around 7:00 a.m. and could see a steady stream of early arrivals. There was little socialization, and everyone pretty much just arrived and went directly to work in their cubicles. Sometime around 9:00 a.m. the place was at full capacity with noise around the coffee maker and copy machine. At 10:00 a.m., most of the conference rooms were at capacity, and the day was fully underway. Very few people were mingling.

At the end of my first week I noticed that almost everyone stayed to their same routine. There were the early birds that arrived at 7:00 a.m., the 8:00 a.m. crowd, and then the 9:00 a.m. everyone else group. What was interesting was there was an office ritual that happened at the end of each day. Around 5:00 p.m. people began to stand up in their cubicles or mingle around the hallway, chatting and watching the people as they departed.

After a few minutes of taking it all in, I observed this ritual wasn't in place to provide a kindly good night to coworkers, but to show who was still in the office past five o'clock. The notion that you were fully committed to the company by staying late each night was important to people. No one wanted to be thought of as someone who left early or on time, because this was considered to be giving minimum effort.

Each day would be the same with little variations. The first to leave were mostly administrative-level employees, followed by people from cubicles located against the far walls and windows. Several people would go out of their way down the cubicle corridor along the far windows to the exit. The only motive would be to be invisible to those staying later. After 6:00 p.m. it was permissible to leave without concern who saw you. You could take your time putting your coat on and use the major hallways to exit. Would you say this behavior is indicative of a balanced work life? All business? Very little social interaction? Putting personal values aside to conform to what you think you're supposed to do?

The consequences of achieving or not achieving a balanced lifestyle are very real and may be never more critical than today. Stressed, overtired, disorganized, overworked, and basically unavailable to people around you are good signs that something is wrong or unbalanced!

Here are some key points for achieving a balanced life:

Be organized and plan. My calendar is actually a combination of calendars that all merge into one calendar of events for me each day: a family item calendar in which Gina and I can add or delete items; a fitness and activity calendar in which only I can add or delete items; and my workday calendar that my executive admin and I can alter. It is critical not to double book or triple book, and when a calendar conflict arises, only you may make the choice about what to do. I've been a busy executive for years, and the best advice I can give you is to understand what balance means to you. It might mean working late on a Thursday night so that you can take Friday off. Or it might mean stopping at 3:00 p.m. to pick up your kids from school. Balance is about your heart and your life. Everyone's interpretation of balance is different. Know what your priorities are. Balance does not entail cramming in every activity possible. My calendar also notes everyone's birthday, anniversary, school event, and little-known tidbits of information. It's amazing when I can bring up things that were done a year ago or significant employee events like employee anniversaries or birthdays. How do you achieve balance?

Review your calendar daily and prioritize work. Set specific boundaries and know what you will and won't do. Know how to say no to something so you can say yes to something better!

Know what your priorities are, especially items that you have committed to others. Then, be willing to pivot. I've observed that time management and updating your list regularly is key.

There is always someone to answer to or something that must be accomplished. There are things we want to do and things we must do. Sometimes you may need help from a superior as to what is most important to work on or deliver, because not all tasks have the same priority. Block actual daily work time for your prioritized items. A big mistake is that people tend to focus on items they like, are interested in, or that are easy to do. That's not prioritizing. That's a recipe for disaster. Taking time to *think* about it really matters!

Take care of yourself, eat healthy, and exercise daily. If

you cannot exercise daily, be sure to nurture yourself with moments of meditation, prayer, and relaxation. You cannot accomplish anything if you're unhealthy.

Identify your values, highlight what's important to you, and write it down. This will be time well spent. Identify your values in four categories: faith, family, finances, and fitness. Under each category decide what activities are most important. These are things that help you keep on course. Perhaps most importantly, these will enable you to establish work-life boundaries. For example, if spending quality family time is highlighted in your values, going out at night to a night club would be counter to that.

Be ready to expect the unexpected. Things will always pop up. You will find yourself heading to a planned meeting when your boss calls you into his or her office to discuss the latest crisis that needs your immediate attention. That's life. In your personal life you must resist worldly distractions and other things that draw your attention away things that matter most to you—your priorities and your values.

All of these are good tips, but without an efficient mindset and a positive mental attitude, chances are weak that balance can be achieved. You must be serious about the management of your time. A big distraction is the amount of your cell phone time usage. My cell provides me weekly and monthly summaries of time spent. The report summarizes the time spent on productivity applications like email and texts versus social media time spent on things like Facebook. I do note my weekly time on my cell phone and try to maintain a healthy time allocation of no more that 10 percent of overall my time. How do people get unbalanced? In my opinion most people just react. They react to their cellphone and email, and that keeps them busy. It's distraction from your ultimate goals.

A big distraction in most people's lives that keeps them from meaningful relationships at home is email or the smartphone notifications. We all get too much email. That's not the problem. The problem is when you develop a habit of constantly checking your email. Unless you're a brain surgeon, don't do it! This is a huge time waster and a big distractor for achieving balance. Consider an alternative. If you allocate time on your calendar devoted to emails, you will find projects and other priorities progressing. Sort your email according to who sent them (e.g., email from senior managers get higher priority).

The point is clearly that achieving balance is an every-day challenge. You must develop good habits and strategies for managing distractions and distractors from impeding progress. Making incremental improvements in balance will undoubtedly reduce stress, improve physical and emotional consequences, and markedly change your relationships at home and at work. I promise if you exercise intentionality in these areas, you'll achieve your definition of balance. As my good friend and coach Tony Jeary says, "Time is the great equalizer. But he who uses that time most effectively gets the best results." This is true at home and at work.

Key Takeaways and Insights #15

Understand Balance

- How does this apply to you?

- What learning can you take away?

- What are you doing to create balance at work? At home?
- Are you taking time to exercise and eat well?
- Is your calendar organized or chaotic? How can you refine it to make it better?
- Do you plan and manage your time, or does it manage you?
- Do you make lists to prioritize your "to-do" lists? List making has been proven to increase one's effectiveness!
- Have you developed the ability to say no to some things in order to say yes to better ones?

Incorporate Music into Your Life

*This Insight offers the realization that we all
need to reenergize and recharge. We need inspiration.
Music is one way to get there.*

Music has played a huge role in my life since early childhood. Looking back, I can remember how it all started with my mother. My earliest memories are of her bringing music into our family. For more than 50 years now, she has been the choir director in her church, and every three or four years she successfully has produced a church musical. She also plays piano and sings.

Her love of music spread though our family. My sister Julie also sings, and my brother Mike plays trumpet in a professional orchestra in Knoxville, Tennessee. I played trumpet in high school and all the way through college. Everyone in my family has made music a significant part of our lives.

To this day I have no problem belting out a tune or singing

along with the radio. Sometimes I may not quite hit the right notes, but my wife, Gina, gives me the look and rescues me. My mother always told me to just make a joyful noise. One of the things I didn't realize when I was practicing during my early instrument training was how learning music would teach me discipline.

I remember playing trumpet, and not just in the band. Sometimes I was the soloist at high school events. I remember being filled with pride as I played the national anthem. I also played "Taps" at funerals for veterans. It would be a cold day in December or January, and I would be playing "Taps" as the cold wind blew. It was an incredible honor, and I took it very seriously.

Today, I find that music still gives me a sense of freedom, erasing worries, and transporting me to a beautiful place. It's a sense of freedom when you drive, listen to music, and hear empowering lyrics. I love to drive down the road with the windows down and the music as loud as it can go. Sometimes it's worship music, sometimes classic '80s rock, and sometimes country. It just depends on my mood. Sometimes it's great just to be quiet and to get lost in your thoughts. Music is great for being quiet because I fill the space with sound and escape from my thoughts.

You may have read the title of this insight and wondered how music fits into your life. But music can be energizing, relaxing, or soothing, and it has been an integral factor for mankind since the earliest biblical days. Music plays a prominent role throughout the Bible. Music inspires me. We all have our favorite soothing songs. Think of ways to incorporate more music into your life, whether it's at work or during a workout.

One of your primary roles as a leader or a parent is to inspire others into action, and that can't be done if you're not inspired yourself. This is where I have found that music steps in to save the day. There have been scientific studies that prove that the music you listen to engages a wide range of neuro-biological systems that affect your psychology. Even athletes use it to enhance their performance. One study at Brunel University revealed that music can enhance endurance by 15 percent. Music is a powerful tool that has both physical and psychological benefits.

That being the case, it only makes sense that a leader would use music as a tool to enhance their own psychology. I know from personal experience that music can inspire and energize. It's where I go when I need a boost or find myself feeling drained.

Everyone needs a way to recharge, especially those in positions of leadership. Without a management system or mechanism, the pressure, stress, and weight of leadership will stifle your ability to lead. Plato said, "Music is a moral law. It gives soul to the universe, wings to the mind, flight to the imagination, and charm and gaiety to life and to everything."

I have found that if you will begin your day in a positive, energized way, it will set the tone for your entire day. Another great benefit about doing that is it is infectious to others. It makes you a catalyst for a ripple effect of positivity.

Through the years, music has been the one place I can go to let go of the pressures of the day and reenergize myself. How do you inspire yourself? Do you have a system or mechanism in place that will help pull you out of the low times? This is something every leader must master, or they will soon crack under the pressure. Outside of prayer, I don't know of anything more effective than music when it comes to solving problems, getting inspired, and rebooting my spirit. I was introduced to the power of music at an early age, and it has served me well throughout my career.

During my formative teenage years, songs like Lynyrd Skynyrd's "Free Bird" helped me get going and inspired in me a mindset. The incredible guitars and the lyrics really spoke to me. I was young, and just like a free bird, I could go anywhere and do anything I wanted. My favorite rock band has always been Boston. Their song "More than a Feeling" was one of my favorites. I remember listening to that song first thing in the morning. That song would put me in a good mood, and I would think, *Today is going to be terrific!* Through college, Sammy Hagar's music would really get me pumped up. And there was also Van Halen. Rock music gets my blood moving and fills me with energy. It takes me to a different place.

You can use music as a trigger to help take you to a happier place. I'm eclectic in my musical tastes with a very broad playlist, so I also like country music. There's a song by Brad Paisley that reminds me of when I first met my wife, Gina. The song is called "Then," and the lyrics really mean a lot to me.

The first couple of verses go like this:

I remember, trying not to stare, the night that I first met you
You had me mesmerized
And three weeks later, in the front porch light
Taking forty-five minutes to kiss goodnight
I hadn't told you yet
But I thought I loved you then

And now you're my whole life
Now you're my whole world.

I just can't believe the way I feel about you girl
Like a river meets the sea
Stronger than it's ever been
We've come so far since that day
And I thought I loved you then

Songs trigger memories, so use that to reboot your mind and to inspire yourself so that you can inspire others.

I told Makayla and Mallory recently, even though they didn't have boyfriends, that I had picked out the song I wanted to play at their wedding for the father-and-daughter dance. It's a song by Heartland called "I Loved Her First." To this day, I tear up whenever that song comes on the radio. The last verse takes me back to when my girls were born.

I loved her first
I held her first
And a place in my heart will always be hers
From the first breath she breathed
When she first smiled at me
I knew the love of a father runs deep
And I prayed that she'd find you someday
But it's still hard to give her away
I loved her first

I love it when artists sing about things that matter. I'm a country boy, so I love when an artist sings about life in the country and gives the world a song that says something meaningful.

As a leader, you must be self-aware enough to know what you need and when you need it. A few years ago, after my divorce, I listened to a lot praise and worship music. Why?

Because it is what I needed at that time. It was a hard time. I needed a lot of time for self, and my children also needed a lot of guidance. I drew strength from the praise of worship music. It helped to shift my mind and heart back onto the things that mattered the most. Singing the song "Here I Am to Worship" fills me with joy and the song is so meaningful to me. It talks about gaining strength by waiting on the Lord, who is our strong deliverer and everlasting God.

> *You are the everlasting God*
> *The Everlasting God*
> *You do not faint*
> *You won't grow weary*
> *Strength will rise as we wait upon the Lord*

The reason I share these things with you is to illustrate how important it is for you to find a way to pull yourself up, get inspired, and be reenergized. It is a must for every person, every leader. Whether it is music, prayer, or exercise, you need something to sustain you and help you recalibrate. Life can be challenging sometimes; there will be difficulties and setbacks. Everyone experiences them; it's only a matter of when.

Music also can have the opposite effect that will pull you down versus lift you up. Choose your music wisely. Sometimes, if you have an emotional connection to a song and maybe that person isn't in your life anymore, it may bring you pain instead of joy. Our brains are triggered in many ways.

What works for me may not work for you. You must find the music or methods that work for you. It's a healthy process to be introspective and reflect on your life. How else will you find out how to keep yourself inspired and ready to face life.

I also play golf and definitely incorporate music into that activity as well. Science has shown that music has the same effect on the brain as exercise because it triggers the release of endorphins. Plus, time out on a beautiful course with the boys and my music makes me feel great.

It's all about finding what works for you, and then developing the patterns and habits that keep you inspired. Learn to say no to certain things and yes to others. Protect your time, your most valuable asset, and protect your mindset.

When you arrive to work, all eyes are on you because you are a leader. When you have honed in on the tools or methods that keep you strong, physically and mentally, you will be equipped to lead others.

I encourage you to find ways to recharge. If you aren't sure where to start, take my advice and start with music. It has been there for me my entire life, and its power to rejuvenate you is nearly unmatched.

You can bet that music will continue to play a large role in my life. So, if you see me exercising out on Katy Trail, you will have no trouble recognizing me. I'll be the one singing louder than I should be with my headphones on. Gina often says to me, "Do you really need to sing when you wear your headphones?" And I just smile and reply, "Yes, I do. Because my mother told me to come make a joyful noise."

"If you get a chance to sit out or dance,
I hope you'll dance" to the music.
—Song by Lee Ann Womack

Key Takeaways and Insights #16

Incorporate Music into Your Life

- How does this apply to you?

- What learning can you take away?

- What kind of music creates positive emotions for you?
- What do you do to recharge, reenergize, and get inspired?
- Music releases endorphins, just as exercise does.
- Music has been shown to have powerful psychological benefits.
- Make a joyful noise!

Nurture Your Health

This Insight offers the value of nurturing your health in three key areas of physical, mental, and spiritual.

You have come a long way through 16 insights into your life. Now is the time to focus on the one that if it isn't giving us trouble, we likely focus on the least.

When you think of being healthy, what comes to mind?

If you're like most people, you think of not being sick or physically restricted in some way. That's true, but being a healthy individual includes a lot more. This is one of my insights, because I realized how important it was long ago to control my stress, manage my emotions, and continually focus my mindset on health.

Wellness matters—there are whole corporate programs devoted to it. Stress kills, obesity kills, cardiovascular disease kills. So why not focus your efforts and mindset on becoming as healthy as you can?

The World Health Organization (WHO) defines health in this way: "a state of complete physical, mental and social well-being and not merely the absence of disease or infirmity."

I have verified the truth of that statement many times in my life. Besides having a physical body in good condition, being healthy includes your relationships, your mind, and spirit. You are not just a body or a mind or spirit. You're all those things, and to be healthy means that all those parts of you must be healthy. Think of this in terms of health management. You must create a system that will help you manage all aspects of your health: physical, mental, and spiritual. All these areas are relevant to living a long and happy life. Everyone wants to look and feel better.

If it helps, you can break down your health management system into three separate components.

Physical Health

This is the most obvious form of health, and in some ways the easiest to manage. Consult with your own physician and develop an exercise program that is right for you. If you already have an exercise routine, that's great and you're ahead of the game. If you're just starting out, remember to start slow and build yourself up a little at a time. Because you are the aggregate of mind, body, and spirit, the health of one area directly affects the health of another. Being physically fit directly impacts your mental health. Exercise reduces stress, eases some forms of depression, improves mental clarity, boosts self-esteem, and more. For me, it's those 10,000 steps daily on Katy Trail, it's 25 miles with my Specialized or a quick trip to the gym.

Mental Health

This area is often overlooked or viewed as less important

than physical health. Nothing could be further from the truth. In fact, if you're not healthy mentally, your physical health will suffer too. Remember, everything is connected. Some attributes of good mental health include

- A sense of happiness
- Ability to laugh and have fun
- Healthy relationships
- Sense of purpose, personally and professionally
- Self-confidence and self-esteem

What are some ways to ensure you remain mentally healthy? One way is through consistent physical exercise and sleep. Another way is spending time with family or friends who support you. Do things that positively impact other people. Music, as we mentioned earlier, is a great way to keep yourself feeling good. Engage in activities that you enjoy.

Spiritual Health

This area is not always so easily defined since we all have different views. I think the bottom line is to recognize that you are part of a bigger picture. What has helped me to become a spiritually healthy person is speaking to God in prayer, listening to praise and worship music, and attending church with friends and family. I mentioned before how I will find time daily to pray and listen to music. Time spent in that way rejuvenates me in ways that I can't duplicate any other way. It is how I integrate my life with something much bigger and meaningful.

The key is to create patterns and habits that will support you in all three areas. These routines may be daily or two to three times a week. The key is consistency.

Think about it. As a leader, if you are strong and healthy in all three of these areas, you will become highly effective and influential. You will be equipped to face challenges and weather any storm. People will be drawn to you, and you will have the ability to build strong, successful teams. You will be fulfilled at home and at work, all because you created a total health management system for your life.

Once again, self-awareness is crucial. Look for signs that your health in any area is beginning to decline. If it's physical, your body may give you signals like an ache or even illness. If your mental health is suffering, you may feel depressed or lack confidence. If you're unhealthy spiritually, you may feel lost and without purpose. Pay attention to these signals and act immediately. Therefore, creating a system is important. In times of need, you will know what actions to take or what decisions to make that will put you back on the right track.

If you need to make significant changes in all areas, it's OK to start slow and work your way up to bigger steps. Baby steps are still progress, and with each step you take, the next one can be bigger. Claim the little victories. Oftentimes, it is small incremental steps that produce sustainable results. So, don't be afraid to start small, just keep going. Remember, you are developing new habits; and these habits will become patterns that will lead to your own customized system for staying healthy and on top of your game.

When you have a healthy body, mind, and spirit, you will experience levels of fulfillment that before may have seemed impossible. Opportunities to be of service will be plentiful, and there will be no end to the many ways you can deploy your talents. Every facet of life will improve. Your relationships, career, finances—every area of your life will see growth. That is a recipe for a long and happy life.

That's important to me because I want to be there for Gina and support her and be her partner for the next 30 or 40 years. I want to be there when my daughters get married, and I want to be able to hold my grandchildren someday. These things are the "why" behind everything I do. What are your compelling reasons to thrive in all areas of your life?

Key Takeaways and Insights #17

Nurture Your Health

• How does this apply to you?

• What learning can you take away?

• How can you develop your own health management system?

• What are the compelling reasons behind your "why"?

• Elements of Health Management: Do you properly nurture all three in your life?
  - ➤ Physical
  - ➤ Mental
  - ➤ Spiritual

Afterword

On that night some 2,000 years ago, Jesus took the bread, and after he had given thanks, he broke it and said to the Twelve, "This is my body, which is broken for you. Do this in remembrance of me." In the same way also he took the cup, after supper, saying, "This cup is the new covenant of my blood which is poured out for many. Do this, as often as you drink it, in remembrance of me" (see 1 Corinthians 11:24–25).

I sincerely hope that some of the Insights from this book can inspire each of us to truly be the body of Christ in this world as we are called to do and to be our best during life's journey.

I would also like to think that in the end I can exit the stage—just as Frank Sinatra did in his song—doing things "My Way."

Mallory, Mark, and Makayla at Churchill Downs for The Kentucky Derby 2015. Our day to watch American Pharoah win the 1st leg of the Triple Crown.

About the Author

Mark is a father to two incredible girls, Makayla and Mallory, a husband to his amazing wife, Gina, and a proven leader with a tenured career of business excellence. He is also a Purdue Boilermaker, a world traveler and adventurer, and a sports junkie. He places faith and family first in his life as he strives to connect people, build strong relationships, and create wins for others in all he does in business, his circle of influence, and local community. He has also just started a new journey with his wife, Gina, via their startup business, M&M Leadership & Advisory LLC. Their new business venture is an innovative leadership think tank and boutique consulting firm.

www.M-MAdvisory.com